My Broken Path Toward Wholeness

Lessons on Redemption, Resilience, Getting Unstuck, and God's Unfailing Love

Brian S Frye with John Troyer

InSpirit Creative

Copyright © 2024 by Brian Frye and InSpirit Creative. All rights reserved.

All Scripture quotations, unless otherwise indicated, are taken from the Holy Bible, New International Version®, NIV®. Copyright ©1973, 1978, 1984, 2011 by Biblica, Inc.™. Used by permission of Zondervan. All rights reserved worldwide. The "NIV" and "New International Version" are trademarks registered in the United States Patent and Trademark Office by Biblica, Inc.™.

No portion of this book may be reproduced in any form without written permission from the publisher or author, except as permitted by U.S. copyright law.

Book Cover by John Troyer.

Published by InSpirit Creative as part of the Wisdom Memoirs series.

This memoir is based on the author's personal recollections and experiences. While every effort has been made to ensure the accuracy of the events, conversations, and details described herein, human memory is inherently subjective and fallible. The author acknowledges that certain events may have been unintentionally misremembered or altered by the passage of time.

The stories and anecdotes contained in this work should be understood as the author's interpretation of past events, filtered through personal perspective and the imperfect lens of memory. They do not purport to be an exact or comprehensive record of historical fact.

Names and identifying details of certain individuals have been changed or left out to protect their privacy.

This work is not intended to serve as a definitive historical account, and readers should not rely on it as such. The author and publisher disclaim any liability for errors, omissions, or differing interpretations of the events described.

Dedication

I have so many people to thank, but I want to specifically thank my wife Amanda, my mother, my sister, and my step-mom, who are and always will be family. We've all been on different journeys through life, but I'm so grateful that we've continued to hang together through all of it. I love all of you so much!

Brian

Introduction

Little White Brian

I've had the whole "walking with Jesus" thing wrong most of my life, I think. I have this little collection in my living room where I have all the knickknacks that people have given me. My sister gave me a little skinny white Jesus on a cross, and I don't usually keep figurines of Jesus lying around, even though I do like Orthodox icons. And I know Jesus was middle eastern, not white. But I just don't like carved images in my living room. I don't know why. Anyway, I put it in my collection because she said that it belonged to my dad.

So I was looking at it one day from across the room, and I heard the Lord say, "Follow me." Then I thought of what he did, how he lived, and how his life is a way of life, from the incarnation to the cross and everything he did. Churches may not have said this directly, but they implied that the gospel that's preached is just about how good your life is going to be and trying to live for that. While I'm finding that he'll give you peace and joy in the midst of it all, that's not really the point.

The point is laying down your life. He laid down his life in full obedience to the Father. It doesn't mean it's wrong to have the things of life but don't aim for them or preach a gospel that tells people that's what we're going to get - health, wealth, and all these good things. People are going to be angry and lose their faith when they lose those things. They'll think God turned his back on them. That's what I felt in Guatemala.

I've realized that I really was not a good husband in my first marriage. In fact, I'm probably still not a good husband, but at least I'm aware of it now. So, I'm growing in that capacity, and I'm learning to be better at it.

To put it more simply, if I could say it in one word, it's humility. You would think that the cardinal virtue of following Jesus is love, and it is - he is love. That's irrefutable. But humility is the key to everything.

The pinnacle of his life, the very enthronement of his essence and who he was, was the exact opposite of what the world would see as good. His enthronement was his crucifixion. His crown was a crown of thorns. It was like the way up is down.

Skinny white Brian needs to follow the rabbi. He needs to follow the master a little closer and stop thinking that life should be comfortable and good for him and being surprised when bad things happen or when people do you dirty. Because, in the words of my wife

INTRODUCTION

Amanda, that's what they do. She says, "Don't be surprised when people do you dirty. That's what they do."

It reminds me of the beginning and end of the Beatitudes that Jesus talked about. Blessed are the poor in spirit and the meek. Blessed are you when people persecute you and say all kinds of evil against you falsely.

I was having a little campfire with some friends of mine recently. The husband was my best man in my previous marriage—that's how long they've known me and how long we've walked through things together. His wife is Filipina, and they came over. We were having hot dogs, cooking out, and stuff.

She had just gotten back from a mission trip to the Philippines with her church, and she was telling me about all her adventures and showing me on a map the islands and what life was like in different places. I said there was only one place in the Philippines that I would desire to go to, that I've always told the Lord I would go to. She asked what it was, and I said the island of Mindanao.

This is going to be weird, but she said that one of her good friends is friends with Manny Pacquiao, a world-famous boxer who boxed Floyd Mayweather some time back. He works for the government over there and is incredibly rich. He's a Christian. Basically, she insinuated that if I'd go preach on that island, she could get me there and would go with me.

I thought I would go if one of my friends would go with me. He's really into this form of inner healing that brings people face-to-face with Jesus without making it overly religious. That form of evangelism would be helpful there. The reason I would go is because that's the unreached island. It's probably not as dangerous as it used to be, but the Abu Sayyaf, a Muslim extremist group, used to have a stronghold there. They have a Trump-like president over there now that cracks down on everything. I mean, people are going to prison for small amounts of weed. It's insane, but he's making it a different place.

Anyway, I told her about a story of when one of my spiritual fathers donated a truck to me in the US, and I came up from Guatemala to get it. I was going to drive it through Mexico and stay at a mission house, All Nations, in Kansas City. There was a book on the bedside by a lady named Gracia Burnham about her and her husband and how they were kidnapped by the Abu Sayyaf in Mindanao. I devoured that book - it was so fascinating. And then I saw a note in it that she had slept in that bed like a month before. I just felt really incredibly connected. That was the moment I said if I ever go to the Philippines, I'm going to Mindanao.

So if I get an all-expenses-paid ticket to Mindanao, will my friends go with me? I'm not saying God is calling me there, but so far, it's an idea that's a seed, not necessarily something that is ready to give fruit. I didn't expect anything from this conversation. I was leaving it completely raw.

As I'm writing this, today was an amazing day in the Spirit. I prayed for people. One was a lady who was using a calculator on the floor while she was working at Menards. I said, "What are you doing, praying?" Now, I knew she wasn't praying, but she was in a kneeling position. I said, "Hey, can I pray with you?" and I prayed a blessing over her life. She accepted it. I told her part of me was trying to be funny, but the other part wanted her to know that we were really praying to the Lord. Then I got up off the floor and left.

Later, we were doing a job for an elderly lady. We had a great conversation about the Lord, and I connected her to a women's Bible study. It was just so flowing.

There's always a level of reluctance about telling my life story like this. Over the last couple of days, I've come to the realization that you can have the message of the cross without applying it to your life. I have to really apply the cross to my life, and that's what I'm working through right now.

So, I've been asking God to help me overcome. It's not like I look at things in terms of major or minor sin; I don't want anything between him and me. I don't want anything to be able to be like a stone in the garden hose that blocks what God would like to do. For example, I feel like over a significant season of my life, I allowed "gas station drugs" in my life, whether that's nicotine - I wasn't doing illegal things, but if it displeases God, I'm getting rid of that. I've quit, but I haven't quit long.

There are other things. You can get herbal supplements that pretty much act like painkillers and stuff, and they are addictive. So I had to quit doing that. It's easy to justify because things are legal, and you're like, "Oh, I have no arthritis pain when I do this. All I do is eat this herb or whatever it is." But I don't feel like God wants me to be dependent on anything. He doesn't want me to be enslaved to anything. And so that's the issue in my life that I'm aware of. I'm sure there are a million other issues that I'm blind to.

I want to be able to say that I have victory in my life and that I walk at a level of victory. But it's not always like that. I'm not saying I've got it all figured out, and I'm not here to tell you how you should live. It's more that I've had the message of the cross in my life for a long time, but truly living it out has been a real journey of walking through that brokenness and getting a picture of what that means.

Throughout this book, I'll be sharing my journey of brokenness, struggle, and redemption. It's a story of how God met me in my darkest moments, even when I felt furthest from Him, and how He has been transforming me from the inside out. The path hasn't been easy, and there have been many times when I've stumbled and fallen; through it all, I've learned invaluable lessons about what it truly means to follow Jesus.

Again, what you'll encounter in these pages is the idea of humility. As I mentioned earlier, love is undoubtedly a cardinal virtue of the Christian faith, but I've come to realize that humility is the key that unlocks the door to a deeper, more authentic relationship with God. It's about laying down our own desires, our own comforts, and our own agendas, and surrendering completely to His will.

Another important thread woven throughout this story is the power of the cross. It's not just a symbol or a nice idea; it's a way of life. Just as Jesus willingly took up the cross and laid down His life in obedience to the Father, we, too, are called to die to ourselves daily. This isn't easy, and it often involves facing our deepest fears, confronting our darkest shadows, and letting go of the things we cling to for comfort and security.

But here's the beautiful truth: when we embrace the way of the cross, we discover a love, peace, and freedom that surpasses anything the world can offer. We find our true identity as beloved children of God, and we begin to see everything - even the most painful and challenging experiences - through the lens of His redeeming grace.

My journey has taken me from the depths of addiction, crime, and incarceration to the mission fields of

Guatemala and beyond. I've become arrogant in spiritual pride and experienced the lows of brokenness and despair. I've wrestled with doubts, fears, and anger toward God, and I've had to confront the ugliest parts of myself. But through it all, I've discovered that God is faithful, and His love never fails.

I've also learned the importance of community and accountability. None of us are meant to walk this path alone. We need brothers and sisters who will speak the truth to us, even when it's hard to hear. We need mentors and spiritual fathers and mothers who will guide us and help us grow in our faith. And we need to be willing to be vulnerable and honest about our struggles and failures, knowing that there is no condemnation for those who are in Christ Jesus.

So why am I sharing my story? I believe that God can use even the most broken and messy stories for His glory. I believe that by being honest about my own struggles and failures, I can offer hope and encouragement to others who may be facing similar challenges. I believe that by pointing to Jesus and the power of His love, I can help others discover the truth that has changed my life: that in Him, we find our true identity, purpose, and freedom.

As you read these pages, my prayer is that you will encounter the living God who meets us in our brokenness and transforms us by His grace. May you be inspired to take up your cross daily and follow Him, even when the path is difficult and the way seems unclear. And may you discover, as I have, that humility, surrender, and obedience lead to abundant life.

Chapter 1

Roots and Resilience

The Shaping of a Childhood

As I begin, I feel it's important to go back to my childhood to give you a glimpse into the experiences and relationships that shaped my early life. Our childhood and family dynamics play a significant role in the person we become, and my journey is no exception. By sharing these early chapters of my life, I hope to provide context for the choices I made and the paths I took, both the broken ones and those that led to healing and wholeness.

My early childhood was spent in Central Michigan, living in small towns like Alma and Carson City. My father worked a lot - 12 to 16-hour days, and sometimes he would take long trips and be gone. So, I was raised largely by my mother. She was a great mom - incredibly nurturing and compassionate. I could tell she had fear in her life, but she was the best mom I could have ever asked for.

We moved quite a bit as my dad would do different jobs. He might be a maintenance man for an apartment complex, and then he'd keep bouncing back and forth doing masonry because that was the family trade. But I don't think he really wanted to do it – it was really hard work. He was a heavy alcoholic and on drugs, but since he wasn't home much, I didn't see that part of him.

I do have a faint memory from when I was maybe five or six years old, that he was in a car accident that almost took his life. They had to open up his throat and put a tracheotomy tube in so he could breathe. I think that was probably the first time, as he told me later in life, that he asked God to let him live so that he could raise his son. He quit drinking after that – I never saw him out of control drunk again.

Moving around meant I went to different elementary schools. I remember being kind of a timid kid and being afraid of people. I was either too young or too old; I particularly remember this young fives program where they put me into kindergarten early. But that's basically my memory. I just remember being fearful when I was a little kid—very timid and afraid of things.

I had good relationships with my cousins, though. We had a pretty large family, and during different seasons, I grew up with a lot of my cousins. We were pretty close.

One cousin would beat me up a lot, but then his sister would protect me. She was my guardian.

My mother was raised Catholic. They got kicked out of the church when she was 12 because her parents got divorced, and that was a big deal to the church at that time. But she would pray with me before I went to bed. She would pray, "Now I lay me down to sleep, I pray to the Lord my soul to keep." When I turned seven or eight, we moved to Goshen, Indiana.

They never took us to church, but when this blue bus came through our neighborhood from the little octagon Pentecostal church by the McDonald's in Goshen, she would say, "Do you want to go?" and we would jump on the bus and go. I remember that, as a little kid, the people were very nice. I remember milk and peanut butter sandwiches. I was a nuisance, and they tried their best to be kind to me. Those are my earliest memories of anything that had to do with God. I was around eight years old.

I used to spend some of my summers in Pineville, Kentucky, with my dad's side of the family. His mom and dad were from Appalachia. We'd spend a lot of time running around the mountains and enjoying the outdoors. I learned a lot from my grandmother - she was a great storyteller and would tell really scary stories to scare us. Neither of my grandparents were believers, but both of my great-grandmothers were. I knew both of my great-grandmothers, and they were both godly women. One of my great-grandmothers raised everyone else's kids and was a real role model of what it meant to follow Jesus.

Through a little kid's eyes, she was just very loving. She continually had her oven and stove going, feeding people. If you caught her in her spare time when she wasn't taking care of everyone else, she'd be reading her Bible. She just radiated peace. She would discipline, but it was out of love. There was a different motivation behind her discipline than some people who would just get irritated and want you to conform and stop being a nuisance. You can feel a different energy behind people's discipline.

I had good cousins and family members who definitely saw me. I had one cousin who I constantly shadowed. He was a foot taller than me, and he would teach me to go out, hunt, trap, and be in the woods. We'd get in a lot of mischief, and we would be kind of rotten together. He got in trouble before me and would write me letters from prison as a teenager, explaining the ins and outs of prison life and how to survive and function in a setting like that. He always told me, "Don't come here, don't come here." To me, he was one of my heroes when I was a kid, even though he was only two or three years older than me. But he taught me to steal. We would steal anything that could be lifted. So, it wasn't all good things that I learned.

I feel like some of my family's culture was deeply grounded in me and has made me the person that I am. They offered a high level of hospitality and accepted people that most people wouldn't accept. They live out that southern hospitality thing.

But there were also some really difficult things. As I said before, one cousin used to beat me up. Our parents would leave us with people they probably shouldn't have, maybe out of lack of discernment or because of necessity. There was this older lady who was our babysitter who exposed us to all sorts of horrible things. I have repressed memories about many of those things, but sometimes, I'll remember a little snippet. I discovered this a year or two ago, and it's the first time that I learned repressed memories were a thing. So I don't really know what happened, but I've learned about some of those things from others. I've come to believe it must be true because I hear it from multiple sources.

The cousin who was a jerk to me as a kid went on to hurt other kids, his own siblings, in even worse ways. I don't know what he did to his brothers. But I went and visited one of his brothers a few years ago. The only way some of my distant cousins and I can really interact with all those memories is when we drink together. So we were drinking, but God used that moment to fill in some more parts of my story.

This cousin, who had been hurting everybody, spent most of his adult life in prison because he was just so harmful to everybody. He spent many years in solitary confinement. It ruined his life, and he ruined a lot of other people's lives. When I spent time talking to his younger brother, I learned he had gone to war with the express purpose of wanting to kill people. I asked him what he was going to do in the military, hoping that he was going to stay off of the front lines. He responded, infantry. I want to kill people. He had a lot of hatred and anger. When he came back, we celebrated, like our family does when someone comes home from the military. But when I was alone with him, I asked if he still wanted to kill people, and he looked away and said no. Whatever happened over there, it had changed him.

This cousin considers me and my sister his only true family. He doesn't even like some of the others in his family, I assume because they couldn't protect him. So we were having some beers, and I told him, "I know when that evil came into your brother." He said, "What?" and I told him the story about the babysitter. He thanked me and said his whole life made more sense. We had a real heart-to-heart over it.

Two days before I went to visit him, I had sent him a photo of him and me as little kids sitting outside of a tent. I sent it as a reminder that he's never been alone. He said, "You know that photo you sent me?" I said, "Yeah." Then he said, "That's one of the times I remember you were the one hurting me." I don't remember that, but I don't doubt it.

I was so scrambled in my brain that things could happen in life that I did not remember. So I asked a new acquaintance to get coffee with me, and I basically told him what was going on. I told him I couldn't stop drinking because I was freaking out over this. He looked at me and said, "Yeah, that's not a sin issue." I said, "What?" He said, "It's an identity issue." Just the way he described it was like a key that unlocked my mind. I walked away, free from the pain and shame. I loved this guy's wisdom, and that's when I decided I wanted to keep hanging with this guy. That's when he and I became friends.

So I grew up in a family system, whether generational or introduced by a babysitter, where we had an abusive environment among the kids with each other. With the unmonitored nature of where things were, it was bad. It hurt a lot of people and had a lot of devastating effects on everyone. I don't remember a lot of it, but somehow, it became part of me and my life. I had to sort that out throughout the years: what did it all mean?

As I reflect on my childhood experiences, I see that there were still those flashes of light: experiences of beauty and truth and goodness. I'm reminded of the words in Psalm 139:13-14, "For you formed my inmost being; you knit me together in my mother's womb. I praise you because I am fearfully and wonderfully made; your works are wonderful, I know that full well." Even in the midst of the brokenness and pain, God was there, forming and shaping me, knowing every part of my story.

It's not easy to look back on the trauma and dysfunction, but I've come to understand that our identity isn't found in what was done to us or even what we've done. In 2 Corinthians 5:17, Paul writes, "Therefore, if anyone is in Christ, the new creation has come: The old has gone, the new is here!" This is the hope and the promise that I've learned to hold on to - that in Christ, we can be made new, no matter our past.

As I continue to unpack my own childhood and the experiences that have shaped me, I find myself bringing them before the Lord. I'm learning to allow him to shine his light into those dark and painful places and begin the work of healing and restoration. It's a journey, but I'm finding that he is able to redeem even the most broken parts of our stories and use them for his purposes.

***

Discussion Questions

Coffee Cup Questions:

1. What are some of your earliest childhood memories, and how do you think they've influenced the person you are today?

2. Did you move frequently as a child or stay in one place? How did that impact your sense of stability and belonging?

Wisdom Questions:

1. In what ways do you see the impact of family dynamics and generational patterns in your own life? How can we begin to break free from unhealthy cycles?

2. Brian's great-grandmother was a powerful example of what it means to follow Jesus. Who has been a spiritual role model in your life, and what did you learn from them?

3. How can we learn to see ourselves as God sees us, rather than being defined by our past experiences or traumas?

Application Questions:

1. Is there a specific childhood experience or memory that you feel God is calling you to bring

before him for healing and restoration? What steps can you take to begin that process?

2. Brian's family culture emphasized hospitality and accepting people that others wouldn't. How can we cultivate a heart of compassion and acceptance in our own lives, even towards those who are different from us?

3. What is one practical way you can begin to embrace your identity as a new creation in Christ this week, regardless of your past?

Chapter 2

Descending into Darkness

The Allure of Addiction and Crime

There was a point where things got really different. I noticed a big change in my life when I was about twelve years old. My mother was displeased that my dad smoked pot in front of us. During my entire childhood, I really didn't understand what marijuana was and didn't see an issue with it. For my mom, it was a big deal, along with a number of other things.

She had a lot of baggage from their whole relationship, both when dating and in marriage. He had continuously cheated on her - he was a womanizer. He was dealing with his own baggage in sinful and wrong ways, and she never really forgot about that and how their relationship was. So when she found an out, she left. And my stability in life left with her.

I remember her leaving and my dad standing in the kitchen with the oven open. He had turned it on, and he was just crying. I knew that he was trying to kill himself, but I was standing right there. That was the moment I felt I needed to live with him to keep him alive.

At that point, life took a different trajectory for me. I already couldn't really make sense of it that well, and all of this put me over the edge. So I began to help myself to his marijuana and anything else lying around. That made me a pretty popular kid in the neighborhood because I always had marijuana. It started there.

And then I found alcohol and started drinking. I found that the things I was afraid of would go away if I drank alcohol, and I could be very bold and do pretty brazen things. It became a way of overcoming the shyness from being younger – my form of liquid courage.

In addition to that, I started robbing houses. The thing I was looking for was guns, to feel like I had a sense of control or a sense of power because I felt completely powerless. I would have guns on me and things like that from a pretty young age, and I was not responsible enough to have them.

Eventually, this life that I had been living - smoking marijuana, doing drugs, drinking, and robbing a few houses - caught up with me. I was a pretty dumb criminal, so I got caught after a short period of time. At sixteen, I was arrested and charged with two B felony burglaries. I was facing six to forty years. When I heard forty years, that was a pretty terrifying thought. We didn't understand the legal system or the justice system. I knew I did it, so I pretty much admitted to it. But I didn't know how big or bad the consequences would be.

They ended up charging me as an adult, but they didn't sentence me permanently to prison. They put me out on a suspended sentence, meaning that if I continued to do okay, then I might not have to go to prison. But by that time, I was addicted to drugs and alcohol. I couldn't pass urine screens and things like that, so I ended up getting sentenced to 8 years, which meant I needed to do four. I did all that time on the installment plan. I would go to jail for maybe six months, and then they would let me back out on probation, and then I would mess up again, and they would give me a year and a half. Then I messed up again, and they gave me two and a half years, at which point my sentence was basically completed.

I was around sixteen when I went to jail for the first time, and I was in there for maybe a month. That was pretty terrifying. I was around seventeen when I first went to prison and did a year and a half.

As far as people intervening in my life and introducing God to me as a teenager, most people saw me as a nuisance and would brush me off. They probably had good intentions, but they didn't know what to do with me. Before I got in trouble with the law, the principal of the middle school told my parents that I was already running with gangs, already dangerous, and that I would be in prison before I was eighteen years old. That's how a lot of people had seen me.

But there were people that God put in my life. I had a girlfriend when I was fourteen who took me to a youth group a few times. So I would be around believers then, but I really had no interest in God. I remember that I would just go to hang out with my girlfriend, and sometimes, we wouldn't even be in the building. We'd be off by ourselves. But there were people like that in my life who had invited me to church.

When I was probably about fourteen years old, my father had a significant God encounter that changed his life. I didn't know how poor we were at the time. I knew we weren't well off, but I didn't know there was any risk of going without food. But my dad knew, and one night, he lay in bed and said, "I'd sell my soul for a million dollars. I don't know how I'm gonna feed these kids." Out of fear, he uttered those words.

Two weeks later, on a Saturday night, we were watching TV, and the Hoosier Millionaire show made an announcement. They called my dad's name to go on the show in Indianapolis. My dad's sister, who used to see a psychic, got the four numbers that would have been the winning numbers from her and handed them to my dad. He went down to Indianapolis terrified. In the hotel room, he cried out to God, and God met him there.

My father came back from Indianapolis and was a totally different person. All he would talk about was Jesus. Everybody thought he went nuts because he didn't get the million dollars, but they didn't understand what had really happened there. My dad became a Christian when I was fourteen, but I agreed with everybody else. I thought he went nuts.

God spoke to my dad and gave him different numbers. He said, "You're going to go home pretty much broke, but you're going to serve me for the rest of your life." My dad only got about $3,000 or $5,000, which is about the least you can get. But God chose the right numbers that were best for him. He came back on fire for God and chased off a lot of his drug buddies because they didn't want to hear about Jesus.

It was a few more years until I had my own encounter with God. I was still dealing with everything over the divorce. I would literally be expelled from school every year, so I would have to change schools. Around the time my dad got saved, I moved to Elkhart to live with my mom and my stepdad. He was a great guy and taught me a lot. He was probably one of the healthier individuals in my life up to that point.

But my mom was a very heavy alcoholic during those years. I don't think she could live with what she had done leaving my dad and how it was affecting us. She drank really heavily, and I didn't want to be around her. So I found my family in the streets. I had a group of friends, and we raised each other in a very dysfunctional environment, whether it was staying out camping for week-long trips at Rainbow Farm (run by pro-marijuana activists) or being raised by hippies and people who did drugs and lived different lifestyles. My friends were about 90% white, with the occasional Native American or black friend, but predominantly white.

Honestly, I didn't have a very good interaction or relationship with other ethnicities as a teenager, having been raised in the midst of hostility on the south side of Elkhart. I had to fight my way out of the Pierre Moran Middle School parking lot on a regular basis for a year or two. At that time, I didn't like black people. But God took that out of me in one moment, one encounter, one zap, when I was in jail.

It started when I was assaulted in jail. In jail, people are separated by race. I was in a room with all white people. There was another room that had black people, and then you had the day room, which was Hispanic. I was sitting with the white people where I was supposed to (I thought). There were a couple of white guys doing meth. When the meth wore off, I was sleeping on a bunk. The guy decided it would be a good idea to just start punching me in the face while I was sleeping. I hadn't done anything to him.

I jumped out of my bed and looked around. All I saw was a bunch of white faces looking back at me. I thought to myself, they just sat there watching somebody who was sleeping get assaulted and did nothing to step in or say that's not right. So I got up and left for the day room to sit with the Hispanics, just trying to gather my thoughts.

Then, all of a sudden, out of the room where all the black people were, a guy said, "Hey, come here." I went over and started talking to him. He said, "Come in here," and I went into their room. They surrounded me and asked, "Did what we think just happened to you happen to you in there? Did he just attack you while you were sleeping?" I said, "Yeah." They asked, "You want us to handle that?"

In that second, any semblance or piece of racism that could have been within me left. I wasn't raised to be racist, but I became one as I was getting beat up for the color of my skin. At a young age, I decided that I didn't like most black people. I had a few black friends. But in that moment in jail, those guys came together and chose to have my back. It reminded me of what my dad always said. He grew up in inner-city Detroit in the '60s and '70s and always told me there's good and bad in every group and don't make it about the whole group. I found that to be true. He had to fight his way through high school until he learned how to defend himself. He was also picked on because he was white.

These experiences were all at the old Elkhart County Jail, the downtown one, which at the time was massively overcrowded. The first time I went to prison, I was only classified as a Level 2. There are five levels, and Level 2 is still pretty low security. I went to a lower security facility outside the walls of the Indiana State Penitentiary in Michigan City. It's called Lakeside. Most people in low-security facilities want to stay there, so they won't usually assault you or do a whole lot of fighting. However, they may test you to see if you'll defend yourself. It was bad, but I guess it was not bad enough to make me want to change. I didn't enjoy being gone for a year and a half.

Before I went to prison, I was sent to a place down by Indianapolis in Plainfield called the Regional Diagnostic Center (RDC). I spent three to four weeks there, and I was with everyone - the murderers, the rapists. I was locked down 22-23 hours a day in a cell with one other person. I never knew who I was going to be with. That's pretty scary. If you watch prison movies, it's kind of what you might see there - being locked in the cell all the time. I got a taste of that before I went to the "good prison."

Going back to the youth group stuff - my girlfriend's mom had invited me to a church in Elkhart, Calvary Assembly. I remember sitting there, and a young man seemed to take an interest in me. He asked me a lot of questions about what kind of music I liked. I told him some rock, some rap. He started digging through all these CDs, which were kind of Christian alternatives to those genres. He just kept handing me CDs, probably like 20 or more in a shoebox. I could tell they were his CDs. I'm not going to say there was any reluctance for him to give them, but I could tell it meant something to him to give me those CDs. That marked me because I thought there was no reason people should be that generous or put themselves out there like that.

The second experience I had was when I was probably 16, working at Walmart. There was a girl named Laura. I wasn't nice to her. I would tease her a bit, but I wasn't a very nice guy in that season of life. Anyway, she invited me to church, and it kind of shocked me that she would invite me. So I went there a few times, and it just so happens that it was Living Faith, the church that would eventually become a big part of my life. I remember meeting Malcolm Webber, the pastor. He gave me a book. I liked the church; I just didn't stay grounded there. I was much more interested in girls and drugs and living for myself. So, I didn't stay rooted there at that time.

I wish I could honestly say there was some sort of positive driving force that kept me going during the time dealing with addiction and incarceration. Deep in my heart, I was often depressed. I had a lot of mood swings. Once or twice, I went to Oaklawn and talked to a therapist. The therapist said, "I can't tell if he's bipolar or not because he smokes so much weed every day, so that could be the cause of it." The fact was I really didn't want to live. I hated my life. I was very suicidal to the pit of my being. My goal was to be dead by the age of 25. I was also a little afraid of death, so I never finished the act. But there were often times I wanted to die. My goal was just for the pain to stop, so that's why I said I never really wanted to get old. I thought I would be dead by 25, and I was okay with that. But then I got in those situations in prison, and life was really bad. I didn't want to feel that way either.

I was pretty selfish and just lived for myself. I would use people. I didn't really care about anybody, even my girlfriends. I just wanted what I wanted. I felt I was utterly and completely hopeless. I thought that where I'd found myself was going to be my life forever. I didn't see any way of changing. I had tried to quit using drugs or drinking on my own many times before, but I never had the strength to stay with it. The addiction was a big thing. I was sure I was hopeless.

My living situation was rather complicated. It was like a hornet's nest. At fifteen and sixteen, I was bouncing back and forth between my mom and dad's house, but mostly living with my dad. Eventually, he threw me out, and I was pretty much on my own from age sixteen forward. For most of my life, my parents would be there if I really, really needed them. But they didn't want me influencing my younger siblings and being drunk because I was really demonized. Things would take over in me, and I was scared. I was very out of control. Whatever was operating through me would scare people. So they kicked me out of the house, and I'd live with friends.

I felt I had lost everybody, and I started getting on pain pills and tranquilizers and combining them with alcohol - basically doing what the pills said not to do - I was killing myself that way. My mom was having dreams of me dying, nightmares. In her dream, she'd visit me at my friend's house, and she would come into the living room. She'd say, "Where's Brian?" and they'd point upstairs to my room. In her dream, she'd go in there, and it was icy cold, the curtain was blowing, and I was laying there blue, dead. This was not far off from how I was living. I would take pills and drink and be out for three days.

Some of that time, I would be on the run from the law. One time, I took off to live in the Appalachians for six or nine months with some of my family. That's when I got very heavily addicted to oxycodone.

In jail, you don't have as easy access to drugs. So I basically decided I'm not going to do drugs while I'm in jail. I'm already here, so those would be my clean and sober times.

But I had a realization the second time I was in prison, which was worse than the first. I would see the same people I'd been locked up with coming in and out. I started looking at them, and the realization happened that this was going to be my life. I'm literally going to be in and out of prison my whole life. That thought scared me.

Despite the interventions of caring individuals, such as the kid who generously gave me Christian music CDs and the girl at Walmart who invited me to church, I found myself sinking deeper into a life of addiction and crime. The pain of my parents' divorce, the dysfunction in my family, and the lack of stability in my life were a perfect storm, and I kept seeking escape and a sense of control through drugs, alcohol, and criminal behavior.

The hopelessness I felt was all-consuming. I was trapped in a vicious cycle, unable to break free from the grip of addiction and the destructive patterns that had taken hold of my life. Even when faced with the consequences of my actions, such as incarceration and the fear of a lengthy prison sentence, I struggled to find the motivation to change. The brief moments of sobriety while in jail were overshadowed by the overwhelming despair and the belief that this was my destiny.

Proverbs 13:12 says, "Hope deferred makes the heart sick, but a longing fulfilled is a tree of life." This was so true in my case; the absence of hope left my heart sick and withering. I was unable to see a future beyond the bars of a prison cell and the next high. The temporary relief provided by drugs and alcohol only served to numb the pain, never truly healing the wounds that lay beneath the surface.

Looking back, I can see how God was pursuing me even in my darkest moments. He placed people in my life who showed me glimpses of his love and mercy, even when I was too blinded by my own pain to recognize it. My father's miraculous encounter with God and his transformation was a powerful testimony, even though I dismissed it at the time. The kindness of the guy in the youth group and the girl at Walmart were seeds planted in my heart, waiting for the right moment to take root.

As I continued down the path of self-destruction, God was patiently waiting for me to turn to him. He knew the depths of my pain and the brokenness of my spirit, and he longed to offer me the healing and restoration that only he could provide. It would take time, and it would take hitting rock bottom, but God was not finished with my story.

***

Discussion Questions

Coffee Cup Questions:

1. Have you ever felt like you were stuck in a cycle of destructive behavior, unable to break free? How did that impact your sense of hope for the future?

2. Brian mentioned the kindness of the youth group leader and the girl at Walmart who invited him to church. Can you think of a time when someone showed you unexpected kindness or invited you to church? How did that affect you?

Wisdom Questions:

1. In what ways can unresolved pain and trauma from our past contribute to the development of addictive behaviors or a life of crime? How can we begin to address these underlying issues?

2. Brian's father had a life-changing encounter with God, but Brian initially dismissed it. Why do you think it can be difficult for us to recognize or accept the transformative work of God in the lives of those close to us?

3. The Bible tells us that God is faithful and will always provide a way of escape from temptation (1 Corinthians 10:13). How can we learn to recognize and take hold of those ways of es-

cape, even when we feel trapped in a cycle of addiction or destructive behavior?

Application Questions:

1. Brian's story highlights the importance of surrounding ourselves with people who will speak truth into our lives and point us toward hope. Who are the people in your life that you can turn to for godly wisdom and support? If you don't have those people, what steps can you take to find and cultivate those relationships?

2. If you or someone you know is struggling with addiction, what practical steps can you take to seek help and support? (This could include reaching out to a pastor, counselor, or support group or finding resources for treatment and recovery.)

3. Take a moment to reflect on your own life. Are there any areas where you feel stuck or hopeless? Spend some time in prayer, asking God to reveal his love and grace to you in those areas and to give you the strength and courage to take steps toward healing and freedom.

Chapter 3

The Awakening

Encountering the Living God

I was in prison when this all changed. I said, "God, if you are really real, no games; if you're real and you can change my life, you can get me free, I'll give you everything. I'll do anything." It was at that moment that it was like everything around me - I wasn't sitting in the room anymore. It was like I could see the universe. It was an open-eyed vision or something like that. I heard a voice that spoke to me. It's a voice that I always knew, even though I wouldn't have admitted it. I've found when God speaks, I've always known him. He said, "You've lived your life for yourself. But I'm here to tell you today that my son Jesus Christ is the center of it all, and him you must serve." That's when I had a heart change. I was dethroned, and I realized that life wasn't about me at all; it was about him. That's when I got free. This was in 2003, when I was 21, and I surrendered.

I got up off the floor and began to read the scriptures. I had a Bible, and I started reading it all the time. If there was any kind of chapel service or anything related to Jesus, no matter who was leading it, I would go and learn. This was in the Westville Correctional Facility.

I feel like God spoke to me; he spoke to my spirit in a still small voice, and he led me every step of the way. He taught me what it meant to follow him. He taught me a new way of living.

Different groups would lead chapels. I remember some were pretty harsh and legalistic. One group had this Bible study series, and I did 19 of the 21 studies. When I was told that I was worshiping on the wrong day, had accepted the mark of the beast, and was going to hell, I had a little crisis. So I had to get alone with God, and I cried out for help. He sent a Baptist guy who showed me in the book of Acts they gathered on the first day of the week. Later the Lord showed me the passage in Romans 14 about what one man considers one day sacred and another the next, but let each man be fully convinced in his own heart. So God answered my prayer and walked me out of all that confusion.

I would encounter a lot of cults and sects in prison, even among the prisoners. We had the Rosicrucian Brotherhood, Black Muslims, and Native American beliefs. I just combated that stuff with what I was learning in the Bible. That's how I learned.

I probably did two or three of the Gospel Echoes books. I ran across them and got some pretty good stuff from them. I remember some pretty astonishing people coming in at different times, pretty faith-filled people excited about God. I always thought that was cool. But it was kind of a mixed bag of information available to us.

I don't remember if I was extremely vocal about my initial salvation experience. I just remember having a heart change and my disposition towards people being different. I still felt I needed to be careful who I was around and how I talked to people. But I saw value in people. I knew that God was true; God was real. And if he was real, then I had nothing to be afraid of in the universe. There was no fear from that point forward; I was not afraid of people and what they could do. I still had to operate with a level of wisdom. I had to be a master of reading people when I was in prison. However, an added layer was not just reading people; I could sense their spirit and know who I could trust and who I couldn't trust. But even with people I didn't trust, if I saw the opportunity arise, I'd just tell them whatever God was teaching me that day.

Generally, it was received well. Probably three-fourths of the people in prison feel pretty hopeless, so if I had something positive to say or something that could improve their life, about the same number would take it well. The rest would tell me to go away, get out of their face, and I'd be like, "Alright, cool, see you later." I just knew who to talk to and who not to.

I learned that deep down inside, people all have the same needs. The people who would tell me to go away would later sneak over to talk to me and tell me about what's going on in their life, maybe how they need prayer for their mom. I have a pretty solid memory of a guy who told me to go away. He came army-crawling over to my room in the middle of the night and whispering up at me, "Pray for my mom; she's got cancer." That was a revelation that no matter how hard someone's exterior is or what kind of face they put on, we all have the same needs deep down inside. We need to be loved.

I didn't really have any nicknames in prison. When I was on the streets, I was called "Fish" for a while because the way I drank was not humanly possible. That stuck with me for a time. People would still call me that.

After encountering Jesus, I felt like there was just a sense of purpose given to me. It's funny how sometimes God speaks through the scriptures. You'll see calendars around people's houses, and they might have Jeremiah 29:11 on them. Well, that was one of the first verses I remember being illuminated off the page. I knew God was speaking to me. That may not be what that verse means; it may just be something to put on a calendar, but it sure worked for me. When God said, "I know the plans I have for you," I realized my life was utterly hopeless before I knew him. He gave me hope; he gave me purpose, and he gave me a future. That was one of the biggest changes - he made me hope-filled.

Three months after I came to know him, I felt like God spoke to me. People often brush off when God speaks to them. They think it's just their own thoughts. But it's typically a still, small voice within our spirit. Three months after getting saved, God said that one day, I would serve him in Guatemala. I remember thinking Guatemala was in Africa, and I didn't want to go there because it was hot. But I had a vision of this tree with this taffy-like stuff coming off of it. So, I just thought it was in Africa. But if he said I was going to Guatemala, I was going to Guatemala. He told me that three months into my relationship with him, so I knew that had something to do with my future.

He also told me they were going to let me out of prison early, which was not supposed to happen. But sure enough, it did. Elkhart County started a new community corrections program. They gave you an option - you could either live at the Faith Mission homeless shelter for three months, or you could go home on an ankle bracelet. God told me to cut ties with my past. He said, "Don't go home to your family, minimize contact with your family, don't have anything to do with your friends." He wanted to teach me to listen to his voice, and he wanted to choose who I would be around in the early stages.

THE AWAKENING

So, I went to live at Faith Mission. I remember showing up there at the old center downtown on Main Street. I went downstairs, and there was a pay phone on the wall. There was one TV against one wall with a bunch of chairs facing it and another TV on the other wall with chairs facing it. I don't know if it's by design, a default way to entertain more people - there's a sports TV on one side, and a movie TV on the other, and people fit in where they fit in. It looked exactly like a prison. I remember getting on the pay phone and calling my dad, saying, "Get me out of here; I'm still in prison!" But I endured. I stayed through and did the three months I was supposed to do.

After three months of being there, I had maybe $5,000-6,000 in the bank. I was working hard and thinking there's no reason for me to live at a homeless shelter; this doesn't even make sense. I got up that morning on my 89th day and started looking for an apartment. The whole day, I just felt a heavy weight on my spirit, like I was making the wrong decision. It was totally illogical - I mean, why not get an apartment if you've got money? But I went looking for an apartment all day, even though I felt like something was off about what I was doing.

I got back that night, having not found an apartment. I was sitting up in this dorm room because, by that point, I was in the Training Faithful Men program, so we had a better living situation. As I was sitting there reading my Bible—I still loved to read the Bible all the time even after prison—I felt like the Lord said, "I didn't promise you an easy life, and I didn't promise you that you'd have the path everyone else would have. Foxes have dens, and birds of the air have nests, but the Son of Man has no place to lay his head. I said to follow me. You need to stay put right where you're at." I stayed put. I lived at the Faith Mission for 11 months total and finished the Training Faithful Men program.

I built relationships there, having the personal attention of Charles Mwali and Seth Swihart, who were running the mission at that time. Getting to know those individuals built a solid base for me.

Training Faithful Men had sections on anger, finances, and many other areas. It was based on the 49 commands of Christ in the Sermon on the Mount. We'd focus on one of those commands each week. However, more important than the curriculum was the community. On Monday mornings, we would get up and pray over all the prayer requests the donors would send in. We would pray for the donors and their families. We would have something called a "one-on-one" where we'd spend time with Charles, maybe for an hour or two a week. He was a deeply spiritual man. He grew up in Zambia, he was from Africa, and he was a pretty deep well.

When we would meet together, we'd just sit across from a table, and he'd have his hands out. I'd put my hands in his, and we'd sit there in silence for just a few minutes. Then, we would talk about whatever was going on in life or where we were going.

I appreciated the attention, being seen, being valued. I appreciated the opportunity to know somebody from the other side of the earth who walked deeply with the Lord and had a greater understanding of who God was than maybe I did.

The hand-holding was healing and didn't feel awkward. Charles modeled things well for me, showing me what it could look like to work in an environment like that. I knew I was supposed to go to Guatemala at some point, so I looked to him as an example of what a Christian leader could look like. He modeled that really well. There was nothing in his character that I could point to or criticize. Even his anger - you wouldn't see it, but you could sometimes feel it. He was a very good example of what it meant to follow the Lord.

About the 10th month of my being there, I felt like God was putting it on my heart to be part of a regular local church. At Faith Mission, they had chapels, so that was my church and community. They would have a lot of different groups come in, mostly Mennonite and Amish. At that time, I wouldn't have been able to tell who was who or understood anything about how churches work. But I remember them coming in and singing beautiful songs with four-part harmony and bringing big casseroles. We liked it when the Mennonites and Amish came in versus some other groups whose food wasn't as good. That was my understanding of church while I was at Faith Mission.

I felt like God said it's time for you to find a church that you're going to go to outside of this place. He led me to Living Faith, the one I had gone to years before, at Benham and Hively. I felt like God told me that was the church I was supposed to go to. So I started going there every time the door was open - Wednesday night, Sunday night, Sunday morning, I was there. Charles went with me the first or second time to meet the pastor and at least check it out to transition me into that season. Once it was time for me to go, Charles remained a friend. He still is to this day. If I stop at Faith Mission today to have lunch with the community or something, I can meet with Charles. I've met with him probably once every four or five years to catch up. Not all the time, but he's still loosely part of my life.

My encounter with God in prison was a turning point that changed everything. It wasn't just a one-time event, but the start of a journey where I began to discover who God really is and learn how to follow Him. This awakening opened my eyes to God's presence, His love, and His purpose for my life in a way I had never experienced before.

As I dove into reading the Bible and praying, I started to feel a new kind of freedom and hope. The addiction and hopelessness that had controlled me for so long began to lose their grip. I was living out what Paul wrote in 2

Corinthians 5:17, "Therefore, if anyone is in Christ, the new creation has come: The old has gone, the new is here!" It wasn't just words on a page anymore; it was my reality.

I also began to recognize God's voice more clearly and found myself willing to obey, even when it didn't make sense logically. When God told me to stay at Faith Mission instead of getting my own apartment, I chose to trust and obey, even though it seemed counterintuitive. This decision led to deeper growth and relationships that would shape my faith journey in ways I couldn't have imagined.

During my time in prison and at Faith Mission, I encountered various religious groups and beliefs. This taught me to dig into the Scriptures and discern truth from error. I discovered that growing spiritually wasn't about following a set of rules or joining the right group, but about having a personal relationship with Jesus Christ. As Jesus said in John 14:6, "I am the way, and the truth, and the life. No one comes to the Father except through me."

Through all of this, I found myself developing a growing compassion for others. I realized that everyone, no matter how tough they might appear on the outside, is deeply in need of God's love. Just as God had looked past my own rough exterior and seen someone He loved, I learned to look beyond the surface and see the hurting, broken hearts in others.

***

Discussion Questions

Coffee Cup Questions:

1. Have you ever had a moment or season in your life where you felt like you encountered God in a new or profound way? What was that experience like for you?

2. Brian found that reading the Bible and prayer were essential to his spiritual growth. What spiritual practices or disciplines have been most meaningful in your own faith journey?

Wisdom Questions:

1. How can we discern between genuine spiritual experiences and counterfeit or misguided beliefs, especially when encountering different religious groups or ideas?

2. Brian learned that obedience to God often involves trusting him even when it doesn't make logical sense. In what areas of your life might God be calling you to step out in faith and obedience, even if it feels counterintuitive?

3. Spiritual awakening often leads to a greater

compassion for others and a desire to share God's love. How can we cultivate a heart that sees people as God sees them, looking past the surface to the deeper needs beneath?

Application Questions:

1. Take some time to reflect on your own spiritual journey. Are there any areas where you sense God inviting you to go deeper in your relationship with him?

2. Is there someone in your life who seems "hard" or "tough" on the outside but may be hurting and in need of God's love? Pray for them this week, and ask God to show you ways you can extend compassion and care.

3. Brian's obedience to God's leading, even when it felt illogical, led to significant growth and blessing in his life. Is there an area where you sense God calling you to trust and obey him, even if it feels uncomfortable or doesn't make sense? Take a step of faith this week and trust him to guide and provide.

Chapter 4

Mentors and Maturity

Growing in Faith and Character

I had a lot of mentors at Living Faith, but there were several primary ones that made a deep impact on my life.

I have to start with Malcolm Webber, the pastor. He was a very deeply spiritual guy and very serious. He would laugh if you said something crazy to him, which I did often. At the same time, he would stay on his square and was pretty focused on what God was doing. He was very much about the Father's business and committed his life to following God. He modeled a passionate pursuit of God, and taught me about staying focused on total union with Christ, walking in conscious contact with Jesus is the source of all our lives and ministry. It all flows from Jesus; to him, through him, for him are

MENTORS AND MATURITY

all things, all for his Glory. Malcolm modeled what a life abandoned to God looked like, and he was a deep well. He truly sought first the heart of God. God had told me to "learn all I could from that man." In many ways, he was my spiritual father, introducing me to a breadth of writers and inspiring me in amazing ways.

Then, there were people who were more pastoral on staff, like Gary Yordy. He was a good mentor to me. He cared more about the family aspect of the church and would take care of families' health, finances, and other things like that. He was probably more like the accountant, but he functioned as a pastor, too.

And then there was Bill Frisbie. I had a season of doing some pastoral work under him, just assisting, nothing super official. It was more like, "Hey, there's this thing going on over here, could you help me with that?"

Ben Stoffel was a younger man; I saw him as the chosen one. He was leading a program called Connexions and later became the pastor of the church after Malcolm had moved on. But he worked very closely with me. He was leading the youth and young adult group when I first started.

This is where my discipleship journey within the church kicked into high gear. I was attending youth group because anytime the doors were open, I was there - Wednesday night, Sunday night, and Sunday morning. I was there all the time. If the building was open and I wasn't at work, I wanted to be in the building. I wanted to be there in the auditorium or somewhere else, spending time with God.

At that time, I had different jobs. Sometimes, I went back and worked with my dad if I didn't have anything else going on, but I also worked in factories.

My relationship with my dad was good at this point. He was super proud of me that I'd come to the Lord. His deepest prayers had been answered. So, in spite of everything, our relationship was always good. It was really good with my mom as well during that time. We had a rocky couple of years when she was drinking. After two or three years of that, she went through her own hardships. But we've always had a good relationship, and it's just gotten better as we've gotten older. My father passed into eternity in 2016, but my mom is still alive today. She's one of my best friends, and it's cool that now, as adults, we relate on an adult level. She calls me, and we share deeply about the Lord and how he's leading us. Our relationship has never been better.

During this period, my dad and I didn't go do outreach together or pray a whole lot together or anything. But we knew that we were both serving the Lord, so we could talk about God and have that connection. I think the further along I went in my journey, the more proud he was of me and just grateful to God that I was turning out the way I was.

MENTORS AND MATURITY

To backtrack to when I was part of the youth group - this is pretty important as far as the development goes. Ben was the youth pastor at that point in time, and they had a program called Connexions, which was like a Christian version of boot camp. It was just intense - eat, breathe and sleep Jesus. You'd be given a host family, assigned an intercessor, and a pastoral coach who was a personal mentor.

Connexions was a nine-month commitment where you couldn't work, you couldn't do anything else. Ben came up to me one night - I was probably 23 years old at the time - and he said, "Hey, I wonder if you'd be interested in doing Connexions." I told him no.

I knew what it was - that if they would teach you that you had to learn to speak or something, then you're going to speak in front of the church. And I wanted no part of that because there are only two things in the universe that I'm afraid of - ticks and public speaking. And there are good reasons for both of them.

Anyway, he asked me if I wanted to do Connexions, and I told him nope, not interested. Then, I went home and spent time with the Lord. I felt like God told me, "What if that's what I want for your life?" I was already enrolled in Ivy Tech and taking general ed classes because I was going to go to seminary. I was going to do something in ministry. When I found out Jesus was real, there was nothing else I cared about in the universe. I just wanted to make him known.

So God told me that I was supposed to do Connexions. I came back the next week and told Ben I wanted to do it.

After a few months or so, I gave up my job and went and lived with a host family and did the nine months of intense boot camp.

They put me in an environment where there would be intense pressure and where I'd have to rely upon the Lord. I'd have a heavy workload - it was like condensing a master's degree into nine months. I probably read 300 books. We'd have big projects that we'd be doing and then learning experiences, which we'd have two or three of a week, lots of time in the Bible, these sessions of just waiting on God where there's no agenda but we just come in to pray and seek God's face and see what he does.

We'd be given challenging assignments built into the learning experiences. If they were teaching me what the gospel was or how to share your faith, then they would send me out to do it. But it would be progressively more intense as the nine months went along, modeled after the idea of Jesus sending out the 72 and then eventually the Great Commission. So, there was always a greater challenge that I was being pushed towards that forced me to rely on God. That was the design of the program.

Looking back, I can see how important mentorship and accountability were in my spiritual growth. The impact of spiritual mentors like Malcolm, Gary, Bill, and Ben was huge. Each of them brought something unique to the table, challenging me to grow, holding me accountable, and showing me what it looks like to follow Christ with passion and integrity.

Proverbs 27:17 says, "Iron sharpens iron, so one person sharpens another." That's exactly what I experienced with these mentors. As I opened up to them about my struggles, I found a safe space to confront these issues head-on. James 5:16 talks about this: "Therefore, confess your sins to one another and pray for one another, that you may be healed. The prayer of a righteous person has great power as it is working." Bringing my struggles into the light and inviting their input and prayers helped me grow and change.

Another big part of this was learning to submit to authority and receive correction. Proverbs 12:1 says, "Whoever loves discipline loves knowledge, but he who hates correction is stupid." When I decided to listen to God's voice and join the Connexions program, even though it meant giving up my job and comfort, it came from a place of wanting to be teachable. My mentors were able to speak truth into my life, even when it was uncomfortable, because I wanted to learn and grow.

It's worth noting that my mentors weren't perfect people who had it all figured out. They were on their own faith journeys, each with their own struggles and areas of growth. We learned from each other, and I think we all grew through the process.

The Connexions program was a turning point for me. It put me in an environment where I had to rely on God, facing intense pressure and a heavy workload. It was like condensing a master's degree into nine months. We read tons of books, did big projects, and had these intense learning experiences. We spent a lot of time in the Bible and in prayer, just seeking God's face.

As the program progressed, we were given more and more challenging assignments. If we learned about sharing our faith, they'd send us out to actually do it. It was all designed to push us further, following Jesus' model of sending out the 72 and then the Great Commission. Each challenge forced me to rely more on God, which was exactly what I needed at that time in my life.

***

Discussion Questions

Coffee Cup Questions:

1. Who has been a significant mentor or spiritual father/mother figure in your own life? What impact did they have on your faith journey?

2. Have you ever been in a mentorship role for someone else? What did you learn through that experience?

Wisdom Questions:

1. Why do you think vulnerability and transparency are such essential components of effective mentorship? What are some of the barriers that can prevent us from being fully authentic with our mentors or mentees?

2. Brian's mentors were able to speak hard truths into his life, even when it was uncomfortable. How can we cultivate a heart that is open to correction and guidance, even when it's challenging?

3. In what ways can pride and self-righteousness hinder our spiritual growth? How can mentorship and accountability help us confront these issues and grow in humility?

Application Questions:

1. If you don't currently have a mentor, what steps can you take this week to prayerfully seek out someone who can speak wisdom and truth into your life?

2. Is there someone in your life who could benefit from your own experiences and wisdom? How can you begin to cultivate a mentorship relationship with them?

3. What is one area of your life where you sense God calling you to deeper growth and transformation? How can you invite the input and prayers of trusted mentors or friends as you seek to take steps forward in this area?

Chapter 5

The Subtle Snare
Confronting Spiritual Pride

During that period of time - going through the programs at Living Faith, being a leader, being called out, up to the time that I was called as a missionary - I had no idea how much pride and self-righteousness dwelt within me as a young man.

I think the self-righteousness had to do with really setting myself apart. It wasn't a deep dependency upon God; it was just gritting myself through, pulling myself up by my bootstraps, doing the right thing, and then being proud that I was doing the right thing, but not knowing that was the case. I was trying to earn my salvation without knowing that I was trying to earn my salvation if that makes sense. Pride and anger were a couple of deep roots in there that I was totally blind to.

But nobody said anything to me about it, so I must have looked pretty humble. But deep in my heart, there was a lot of pride and anger. The only people that would see my anger were the people that I was closest to.

Looking back on that period, the affirmation and recognition by people fed into a growing self-righteousness and spiritual pride. I don't know if people spoke too highly of me - it might have just been in my head that I thought I was somebody special. Malcolm was really good at helping me see what it meant to give God glory in what I did. He saw the dangers of losing humility and being focused on performance and was great at helping me avoid that. He was doing it for my protection.

I remember looking for some sort of affirmation. The first time I spoke at the church, I said a little 5-minute thing that I had really prepared for. It went really well at the first service. At the second service, Malcolm was like, "You guys gotta listen up; this is really good." Then that one didn't go as well. Despite Malcolm's wisdom and efforts, I still let it get to my head.

So, I don't feel like a lot of people puffed up my ego. I think my ego was just internally inflated because I was doing the right thing. I turned into the older brother in the prodigal son story - I was the one slaving for the Lord, doing everything right.

I learned the importance of different kinds of mentors. During Connexions, one of the spiritual fathers I chose was pretty direct - he called me out on my junk, anything he was aware of. So I chose him because I knew he would tell me the truth.

The design of Connexions was to build leaders who don't fail. You'd look around the world and see all these big names failing because of integrity or character issues. So we would try to build people who don't fail. Hearing that now, I can see how the system itself could become a source of spiritual pride. It's a good check for me—my pursuit of wanting the right way, the right thing.

It was based largely on a lot of people having come out of Faith Assembly. There was power in having faith in God and believing him despite your circumstances - without faith it's impossible to please God. In their previous church upbringing from which they'd broken free, there was pride in not watching television or in being really consecrated to the Lord. I had read some of Hobart Freeman's books in prison and enjoyed a large portion of them before even knowing Living Faith had any previous roots there.

I remember one time one of my spiritual fathers really helped me. I was sitting in the church feeling down, wrestling through something. He asked me how I was doing, and I said, "I'm not really doing that well. I'm just wrestling through something." I was going on about me, me, me, I, I. He kind of turned and looked at me and said, "Pretty full of yourself, aren't you?" That ticked me off, but then I stopped and looked at my heart and said,

"I am full of myself." That snapped the self-centeredness right out of me at that moment. I believe that was very much the Holy Spirit.

But in a Christian environment, sometimes you don't notice the water that you're swimming in because you're used to it. It was a better environment than where I'd come from, and there was a lot of good.

I see it in almost every denomination or stream. We see the errors of where we were, but now we're going to fix it, and it's going to be better. This is a new way to do it. Then we see errors there and go to the next thing. But we overcompensate; it's like the swinging of a pendulum. People do it in parenting, religion, everything. The underlying threat is always spiritual pride - "We now know better." So you never actually leave behind the thing that's the real problem, the spiritual pride.

That's the way I've seen it with every denomination and movement. Remember when the Lord was leading the children of Israel by a pillar of cloud or fire - that's the way the whole church has operated. God does something new or reveals an aspect of who he is; there's an emphasis on that facet of his character. Then, people camp around that idea or the person who got the revelation. Fifty years later, they're still singing the same songs, like a little clanging monkey toy still doing the same thing. But by that time, God was no longer seen in the building because the people worshipped what had happened in the past. Instead of following God, They're following the idea of what God did earlier. But the truth is, we can't control the idea or the thing.

Spiritual pride is a subtle but deadly snare that can creep into even the best of intentions. It's the voice that says, "Look at how much you're doing for God, how far you've come, how much better you are than those around you." It's the attitude that takes credit for the work of the Holy Spirit and elevates self above the Savior.

In my own journey, I've had to confront the ugly reality of spiritual pride more times than I'd like to admit. As I grew in my faith and took on leadership roles, it was easy to start believing my own hype. I'd look at how I was living compared to others and think, "I'm really nailing this Christian thing." But that's the deception of spiritual pride - it blinds us to our own brokenness and need for grace.

The Bible is clear about the dangers of pride. Proverbs 16:18 warns, "Pride goes before destruction, a haughty spirit before a fall." James 4:6 reminds us, "God opposes the proud but shows favor to the humble." When we allow pride to take root, we position ourselves in opposition to God himself. We forget that every good thing in us is a result of his grace and mercy, not our own effort or righteousness.

One of the sneakiest ways spiritual pride manifests is in the comparison game. We look at others and think,

"Well, at least I'm not struggling with what they're struggling with," or "I'm doing so much more for God than they are." But this comparative thinking is the opposite of the Gospel. It's not about being better than anyone else; it's about recognizing our shared brokenness and need for a Savior.

Another way spiritual pride shows up is in a lack of teachability and accountability. When we think we've got it all figured out, we close ourselves off to correction and growth. We become defensive when others try to speak truth into our lives, assuming we know better. I have to go back to Proverbs 12:1 again, which says, "Whoever loves discipline loves knowledge, but whoever hates correction is stupid." Ouch. That's a hard pill to swallow, but it's true. We need people in our lives who will lovingly call us out and point us back to Jesus.

So, how do we combat spiritual pride? It starts with honest self-reflection and a willingness to invite God to search our hearts. Psalm 139:23-24 offers a beautiful prayer: "Search me, God, and know my heart; test me and know my anxious thoughts. See if there is any offensive way in me, and lead me in the way everlasting." When we open ourselves up to God's loving scrutiny, He will gently reveal the areas where pride has taken root.

It also involves cultivating a posture of humility and gratitude, acknowledging that every gift, talent, and good thing in our lives is a result of God's grace. As

1 Corinthians 4:7 asks, "What do you have that you did not receive? And if you did receive it, why do you boast as though you did not?" When we live with an awareness of God's unmerited favor, it becomes harder to elevate ourselves above others.

Sometimes, the only solution to spiritual pride is to go through suffering. When the substitutes are taken away, it gives the opportunity to truly depend on God again in a new way.

Finally, combating spiritual pride requires a commitment to community and accountability. We need people in our lives who will lovingly speak the truth to us, even when it's uncomfortable. This is where mentorship and discipleship become so crucial. When we allow others to speak into our lives and call out our blind spots, we position ourselves for true growth and transformation.

May we be people who are quick to recognize and repent of spiritual pride, eager to give God all the glory, and committed to walking in humility and gratitude all the days of our lives. It's a lifelong journey, but it leads to true freedom and joy in Christ.

***

Discussion Questions

Coffee Cup Questions:

1. Can you think of a time when you caught yourself comparing your spiritual journey to someone else's? How did that affect your perspective and attitude?

2. Have you ever been in a church or ministry environment where spiritual pride seemed to be prevalent? What was that experience like, and how did it impact your own faith journey? As you look back now, are you proud you can see it? (Ha, ha, see how easy it is to get hooked?)

Wisdom Questions:

1. Why do you think spiritual pride is so dangerous, and how can it hinder our relationship with God and others?

2. In what ways can our past experiences or church backgrounds contribute to a sense of spiritual pride or self-righteousness? How can we break free from those patterns?

3. What role does gratitude play in combating spiritual pride, and how can we cultivate a more consistently grateful heart?

Application Questions:

1. Take some time this week to prayerfully ask God to search your heart and reveal any areas where spiritual pride may have taken root. What steps can you take to begin to uproot those attitudes and cultivate humility?

2. Is there someone in your life who has permission to speak the truth to you and call out blind spots, even when it's uncomfortable? If not, prayerfully consider who you might invite into that kind of accountability relationship.

3. What is one practical way you can seek to give God glory and credit for the good things in your life this week rather than subtly taking credit for yourself?

Chapter 6

The Call to Go

Stepping Out in Faith and Obedience

My first wife and I were married for three or four years before we went to Guatemala. She volunteered at Connexions, and I worked in a factory for a year. After that year, I would meet with Ben Stoffel once or twice a week, and we would take walks and talk about the Lord. We were friends.

One day, I was running a floor cleaning machine, working the third shift at Menard's, cleaning the place at night. I was pretty miserable and partly wondering if this was it for me. I thought there was more to it. I found myself a little frustrated. One night, I heard God say, "Pray the prayer of Jabez." I thought it was so cliché, but I felt like the Lord told me to do it, so I started praying the prayer of Jabez.

THE CALL TO GO

On day 38 of praying the prayer of Jabez, I went for a walk with Ben Stoffel. He got serious and told me he was moving out of his position as the director of Connexions because they had asked him to come on as one of the pastors of the church. He said there was no better person they saw as suitable for running the program, so they wanted me to pray about being the director.

I took that job and led the school for at least three or four sessions from 2009 to 2012. It was a gradual thing where there was high scrutiny in the first year, and I was really watched and observed. Even in curriculum design, I didn't have the freedom. But gradually, by the second and third year, I was designing the curriculum and calling in the teachers I wanted. It was awesome and so much fun. I was in my sweet spot.

I had responsibility for 8 to 15 people from ages 18 to 35, primarily focusing on the 18 to 25 age range as it was primarily a gap year program for young adults. By the second or third year, I had a lot of autonomy in how to run it. Those were some great years in my life. We were pretty happily married and I loved my work.

I was living squeaky clean, but I had that underlying anger and pride deep down inside of me. It was so well hidden that people around me didn't know, and I was mostly blind to it myself. If my wife knew, she didn't say a whole lot about it. I wasn't physically abusive or verbally abusive. I never directed my anger at her. It was more of a case of swearing or something while I was alone, if I was frustrated, or if something was overwhelming. It would be me in a room by myself, swearing for like 15 minutes, but it was in me.

Sometimes there would be an overwhelming amount of stress from carrying too much stuff, and having to repeatedly face a bunch of fears or something and just the challenges of life. I wasn't very emotionally developed to be able to handle some of that stuff. I could handle it well in front of people, but inside it was crushing me.

Before I continue with the story, I want to mention that Guatemala was a bad word in my house. I knew we were called there, but my wife at the time had a horrible experience in Africa and did not want to go to another country. When she was in Africa, she saw a lot of strange things. It was demonic and heavy.

I didn't see my experience overseas like that because I had a good time. She was a little more aware of the spiritual realm than I was. The first year, she was cool with talking about Guatemala, but it became a point of contention and argument for us. Eventually, I stopped talking about it because I was enjoying Connexions; we were doing well, and I didn't want to fight with her.

One day, while living in a little condo, I was praying in a room when the Lord said, "Get your life in order, get out of debt; you're going to Guatemala." I replied, "God, listen, I'm not going to Guatemala. My wife hates

THE CALL TO GO

Guatemala, and I'm not even going to talk to her anymore about it. You're going to have to tell her we're going to Guatemala because we're not going."

A few minutes later, I came out of the bedroom and found my wife lying on the couch, crying. She looked up at me and said, "He said I need to stop resisting His will and that we're supposed to go." I took that as my sign that God said we were going, and we did not talk about it anymore.

A few weeks later, I asked Malcolm if I could meet with him. I sat down in his office and told him I was going to Guatemala. He asked who was going to handle all my business back here, not meaning Connexions, but paperwork and administrative things. I said, "Well, I hope you do." He replied, "We got you."

Malcolm helped us take care of all of those things so that we could become missionaries. Malcolm had watched me, known me, and we had prayed together a lot. He knew I heard the Lord and saw me speak prophetically in the early days when God would speak through me.

Hearing God speak was actually terrifying. There would be an open mic policy at the church, basically a free-for-all. You'd really have to say something whacked out to be asked not to get on the mic anymore. We would be in worship, and the Lord would say, "Go up to the mic. I want to say something." He would very seldom tell me what it would be ahead of time, and that would terrify me.

I would go up there feeling like everything inside of me wanted to come out. I was so scared, feeling like I was going to soil myself. I was literally terrified most of the time, all the time while I was at the mic in that way. Then I would open my mouth, and he would speak. Eventually, we got a better deal going, where he would usually at least let me know how it was going to begin or give me an impression, but he just spoke through me.

I felt very out of control, and it was terrifying. Looking back, I would pray that I grow to know him, love him, and trust him enough to allow that to happen without having fear. That's how I feel about the whole situation. I'm not going to say it took away my prophetic gift and gave me an evangelistic gift or something, but I almost feel like that.

Malcolm saw me share those prophetic words often. We would be in meetings and prayer meetings, so he knew that I heard from God. If I said I was going to Guatemala, it wasn't in a vacuum. It wasn't like I just felt like I wanted to go to Guatemala.

I told God I wouldn't go to Guatemala without about $10,000. I said that I needed three to six months' worth of living expenses and that I wasn't going there and turning around and coming home right away. Shortly

THE CALL TO GO

after I made my request to the Lord, we got a call from one of my wife's brothers, who had a family business. They hired us to help them coordinate the moving of one factory to another because they had sold the building and wanted to move stuff. We moved away for six months or so, lived with her brother, and worked. We earned $10,000.

We went back home to Indiana and started getting ready to leave for Guatemala, but I still needed a job to keep working because $10,000 was all we had. No one would hire me because of my record as a felon. I literally could not get a job, and there were closed doors everywhere. Over the next three to six months, we spent the $10,000 because we needed to eat and live.

We got down to the bottom of the barrel, and I was trying to make sense of how this was going to work out. As we reached the end of the money and I had lost heart, I got a phone call from the church. The secretary asked me what I wanted to do with the money in the mission account. I thought it was like $300 or something, so I said, "I don't know. Give it to somebody or save it for a trip or something." She said, "No, you don't understand." Now you need to know I had not told anyone how much money I needed before I would go. That was a conversation between God and me. She asked me to come in so she could show me what was there. I went in and saw it was $10,000 to the dime.

God told me, "I don't need you to earn your way. You do what I tell you to do, and I'm providing for you."

Shortly after that, we ended up heading to Guatemala. The fundraising and stuff were easy. We had a couple of parties and made the need known, but it wasn't difficult. People wanted to support us.

The first few months in Guatemala were challenging. Before we went down there as fully committed missionaries, we decided to try it out for maybe three months. We knew a missionary couple, an elderly couple who lived down there, so we went to see if we could help them out for three months and stayed with them.

About two weeks after being there, we got our first outing. I had been to Guatemala before, out in the villages and the sticks where there's no electricity, no running water, just mud huts and poverty. But after two weeks of being there, the missionaries took us out on our first adventure. We went out to the countryside, and a person in our group was really struggling with an issue. It was bad and getting worse and worse the further we got on our five-hour trip.

We showed up at this village, and I was supposed to speak. The situation continued to get worse and was overwhelming. We were sitting on the side of this mud hut, the church building, literally five minutes before I was supposed to walk in there and share a message of hope from God. I reached the end of my rope.

THE CALL TO GO

Up to that time, I had been pretending to be strong, but everything within me snapped and crushed. I was sitting on the side of this mud hut, looking out at a rolling hill. Nobody spoke English except the other missionaries inside. I looked up and yelled vulgarities at God. I was so mad. Then I realized what I had just yelled at God. I collapsed, put my face in my hands, and was broken. I said, "God, did you bring us all the way here for this?"

Then, the Lord directly gave me a solution. I turned and said, "I think we're gonna be alright."

I went in there, and the older missionary translated the message as I shared the importance of knowing God and how to have a daily devotional time. After the message, the missionary said, "Man, that was a really good message."

After we got back in the truck and started heading back towards Guatemala City, I asked the missionary if he knew where we could get the specific medicine God said we needed. He didn't know what that was, and I didn't either. I explained that I thought it was some kind of medication. He called some friends who were more into homeopathic medicine, not even real pharmacists.

When he asked them about the medicine and dosage I had heard, they said, "You're never going to guess, but my daughter got that exact prescription three months ago, and she didn't use them. We have a whole bottle lying here. If you want it, you can have it." We went back, and they gave us the prescription. It helped make things a bit better.

We had initially gone to Guatemala for three months, but we ended up having a difficult time. My wife and I weren't really adapting well, and the older missionary couple really didn't know how to handle it. In hindsight, we were probably more of a burden on them than a blessing. The man mistreated me a few times and was pretty disrespectful. I harbored some resentment in my heart that God had to deal with later, but they just didn't know how to deal with us.

As I reflect on our early experiences in Guatemala, I'm reminded of how God's call to go is often accompanied by challenges and struggles. Stepping out in faith and obedience doesn't guarantee a smooth path; in fact, it often means facing our fears, our weaknesses, and our limitations head-on.

But here's the beautiful thing: it's in those very places of brokenness and inadequacy that we experience God's provision and guidance in profound ways. When we come to the end of ourselves, we discover that he is more than enough. As 2 Corinthians 12:9 says, "But he said to me, 'My grace is sufficient for you, for my power is made perfect in weakness.' Therefore, I will boast all the more gladly of my weaknesses so that the power of Christ may rest upon me."

In our journey to Guatemala, God provided for us in miraculous ways, from the $10,000 we needed to the prescription that brought relief. He was with us in the moments of fear and uncertainty, whispering words of comfort and direction. As Deuteronomy 31:8 reminds us, "The Lord himself goes before you and will be with you; he will never leave you nor forsake you. Do not be afraid; do not be discouraged."

Missionary work is not for the faint of heart. It requires a deep reliance on God, a willingness to step out of our comfort zones, and a commitment to serve others even when it's hard. But as we follow God's leading and trust in his provision, we discover the joy and privilege of being part of his redemptive work in the world.

If you sense God calling you to step out in faith, whether it's to the mission field or to a new area of obedience, know that he is with you every step of the way. He will provide what you need, guide you through the challenges, and use even your weaknesses and struggles for his glory. As Philippians 1:6 promises, "Being confident of this, that he who began a good work in you will carry it on to completion until the day of Christ Jesus."

Are we people who are quick to say "yes" to God's call, trusting in his faithfulness and leaning into his strength? It's in stepping out in obedience that we experience the fullness of his presence and the joy of being part of his unfolding story.

***

Discussion Questions

Coffee Cup Questions:

1. Have you ever sensed God calling you to step out in faith in a specific way? What was that experience like, and how did you respond?

2. Brian and his wife faced significant challenges and struggles in their early days in Guatemala. Can you relate to a time when following God's leading felt difficult or overwhelming? How did you navigate that season?

Wisdom Questions:

1. Why do you think God often calls us to step out of our comfort zones and into places of reliance on him? What do we learn about God and ourselves in those experiences?

2. Brian's missionary group had to confront the reality of struggles that were not solely spiritual in nature but also had other components. How can we develop a more holistic understanding of the challenges people face, and respond with both faith and wisdom?

3. What role does community play in supporting and encouraging us when we step out in faith and obedience? How can we be that kind of support for others?

Application Questions:

1. Is there an area of your life where you sense God calling you to deeper obedience or faith? What practical steps can you take this week to say "yes" to his leading?

2. Brian and his group experienced God's provision in miraculous ways, from the financial support they needed to find the right prescription. Take some time to reflect on your own life and identify specific ways God has provided for you in the past. How can remembering those experiences strengthen your faith for the future?

3. Missionary work, whether in a foreign country or in our own communities, requires a heart of service and a willingness to put others' needs before our own. What is one practical way you can serve someone else this week, even if it requires sacrificing your own comfort or preferences?

Chapter 7

Healing in Community

The Power of Doing It Together

When we went back to Guatemala long term, we felt very alone for the first six months. We actually went to Antigua, Guatemala, which is a touristy place, but it had a lot of Spanish schools, so we went there and started reaching out in small ways. It wasn't much, and we wondered, "What are we doing here?" But we knew we had to learn the language. So, we just found peace in language learning.

I would sit in Central Park in the morning and witness to the tourists. You'd have a lot of Israelis and people from all over the world, from Asia, and I thought it was really cool. But we felt very alone. I had a lot of students from Connexions in that area. But this was after they were done with Connexions. They were back home, got married, and started their lives. They didn't want to hang out with Director Brian. I mean, they entertained me a little every now and again, but we didn't have close relationships with people. So it was just my wife and I during those first six months, and it was pretty lonely. But God put people in our path.

I was a very type A, driven personality. People couldn't keep up with me because I seemed to have a lot of energy. I was trying to prove to myself that I wasn't who I once was and trying to earn the Father's favor because I thought that's what you did. I wasn't secure in His love, so I was very driven and trying to earn His approval. I would run hard. In fact, at one point, I said, "When I die, just put my name on a gravestone and say, 'He ran hard.'" That was my goal in life. Most people couldn't keep up with me, and I didn't stay in step with my wife because I didn't know how to be a good husband. I didn't know how to love her.

We had a really good conversation with Malcolm before we left to be permanent missionaries. He gave us some really good advice. I had my paper and pen ready, and I remember probably point three or something like that, "Stop taking yourself so seriously. You have to learn how to laugh at yourself because there's going to be funny things happening a lot, and you're going to be misunderstood, so don't take it personally." That would pretty much describe my experience.

There were a lot of misunderstandings in Guatemala. There were people with guns on every corner. It was a free-for-all, like the Wild West. If business owners didn't want their shops to get robbed, they needed to hire someone with a shotgun to stand in front of it. There were truckloads of soldiers driving around with M-16s and stuff, but they weren't always disciplined soldiers as might be expected.

My wife and I would be walking on the road, and soldiers would make this little noise at females. It's a very male-dominated society, so they just try to get their attention or make gestures. There would be a truckload of five or six armed soldiers cat-calling my wife right in front of me. I threw my hands up like I was going to fight them. That's kind of what I had to learn to deal with. It was one of the challenging aspects that was there for us.

When we first moved there, we stuck out like sore thumbs. It was a constant comparison. Like a fish in water, we're always in an environment, and we don't always realize that environment because we just live in it. When we get into a new environment, and all the social cues, the culture, the communication, the language, the understanding, and the worldview that shapes their society are completely different, we stuck out badly. But gradually, through rubbing shoulders in a new culture, we learned mannerisms, ways of thinking, and language.

We began to find that culture, as Malcolm said, it's not better or worse, it's just different. We learned that some things are actually better than the way that we grew up. We learned the value and why there is more of a collective mindset. We start taking on their mannerisms, their language, and their way of thinking and some of their values over the course of five years.

Then, when I came back to the US, I didn't really feel like I fit in there anymore. As a way of thinking about it, the US would be a yellow country, and Guatemala is a blue country. When I moved down there, I was just a yellow guy that stuck out like a sore thumb. But then, eventually, I started turning green, and I'm a little more like them. I learned their ways, and then I came back home, and I was green. I didn't fit in here anymore. I adopted the things that I saw that I was part of and the water that I was in. I started to take on those characteristics and those mindsets that I found more valuable.

We're extremely individualistic in the United States, and Guatemala is not as much that way. They find their identity in their community and in their family. Every culture around the world is fear, guilt, or shame-based. That's a negative aspect of the fall, a negative element of the fall. That's our primary motivating thing to get people to act right. The United States is more of a guilt-based culture, and Guatemala is more shame-based.

I would sit there, and I would be meeting my neighbors, and then all of a sudden, their son came in, and the mother said, "This is my son. He's a very bad boy; he drinks alcohol." She's like, "This is my son. He stays out all night drinking with his friends." I looked at her son, and his head went down. He doesn't want to be seen; he's ashamed of his behavior. My wife and I at the time were like, "Why would she do that to her son? That's bogus. Why did she call him out like that?" Really, that was her way of getting him to conform. I don't go around shaming people now, but at least I understand why they did it.

When I first moved there, my eyes were on Jesus. In all the seasons of my life, I'm the most comfortable when my eyes are on Jesus. Even being in prison was good because my eyes were on Jesus. I was closer to Him than I'd ever been because I needed Him for my survival. I was deeply dependent on Him not to get robbed or whatever else could happen.

When you're first learning another language, it's difficult. Your brain is fighting you the whole time. Language and culture are almost interwoven with each other. At least with the Spanish language, the way that they speak has elements of how they live. They're more subtle when they talk to each other. They're not as direct. They're heart people, not head people, and there's more emotion in the language.

The first year that I was speaking Spanish, I was translating in my head. About the time that I stopped translating in my head, all of a sudden it felt like there's not a separate person in me anymore. It just became me and it's naturally who I am. I can stop and speak in Spanish, I can speak in English, and it's the same person now. It was also like that when integrating into the culture.

A lot of my Hispanic tendencies are not as prevalent, but I can still very much relate. If I see somebody from a Latin American country, especially Guatemala, I still feel an intense draw. When I was working at Pollywood (a factory) and I'd meet another Guatemalan, boom, our hearts were knit. We talked about the same places. It's part of who I became.

At first, it felt like I was doing my best to fake it. They're much more formal. They call each other Señor and Señora. The literal translation is Lord and Lordess. There's a lot of formality. When I would go into somebody's house, they would welcome me in.

They don't look at people as much as an individual, but we'd greet the whole family when we came into a room. I'd shake everyone's hand and acknowledge their existence. When I left, I did the same. It's very much ingrained.

At first, it feels foreign and weird, but then it becomes natural and normal. I guess I turn it on and off, depending on who I'm talking to. I have learned to relate to individuals based on what I sense is their way.

The thing that we admire in our culture is a self-made man or woman, the one who's really risen to the top and done great things. But what if, in God's economy, it's more like the incarnation? What if it's more like the cross? What if it's more like serving and loving and caring quietly? Like Paul says in probably 1 Thessalonians, "Make it your ambition to live a quiet life and to work with your hands." What if, in God's economy, things like that are much more important than how big your church is?

As I reflect on our experiences in Guatemala, I'm struck by how community shapes our healing and growth. When we first arrived, my wife and I felt isolated and alone. We were struggling to find our place and connect with people in meaningful ways. But gradually, as we immersed ourselves in the culture and language, as we rubbed shoulders with our neighbors and began to see the world through their eyes, something began to shift.

We discovered the power of a collective mindset and the beauty of finding identity not just in our individual achievements but in our relationships and our shared experiences. Ecclesiastes 4:9-10 says, "Two are better than one because they have a good return for their labor: If either of them falls down, one can help the other up. But pity anyone who falls and has no one to help them up."

I think about the way that mother called out her son's behavior in front of us. At first, it seemed harsh and even cruel. However, as I began to understand the culture more deeply, I realized it was her way of inviting the community to help shape her son's character. There's wisdom in understanding that we need each other and that we're not meant to navigate life's challenges alone.

This is true not just in the context of cross-cultural ministry but in every aspect of our lives. We need people who will speak the truth to us, who will call out our blind spots and help us grow. When we invite others into our journey, when we're willing to be vulnerable and authentic, we open ourselves up to the transformative power of community.

I think about my own marriage and how much I struggled to love my wife well in those early years. I was so focused on my own agenda, on proving myself and earning God's approval, that I often failed to see and meet her needs.

Growth and healing aren't solo endeavors. They happen in the context of relationships, in the daily choice to love and serve one another. 1 John 4:11-12 reminds us, "Dear friends since God so loved us, we also ought to love one another. No one has ever seen God, but if we love one another, God lives in us, and his love is made complete in us."

If you find yourself feeling alone or stuck in your journey of healing and growth, I encourage you to lean into community. Seek out people who will walk alongside you, who will speak truth and grace into your life. Be willing to be vulnerable, to share your struggles and victories. And look for ways to extend that same love and support to others.

As we do this, as we choose to live in the beautiful mess of authentic community, we'll discover the joy and transformation that comes from doing life together. We'll learn to see ourselves and the world around us through new eyes, and we'll experience the healing power of being known and loved just as we are.

May we be a people who embrace the power of together, who choose to live out the incarnational love of Jesus in the context of authentic community, for it's in learning to love and be loved that we find the healing and growth our hearts long for.

***

Discussion Questions

Coffee Cup Questions:

1. Have you ever experienced a season of loneliness or isolation in your own journey? What was that like for you, and how did you navigate that time?

2. Can you think of a time when someone else's perspective or cultural background helped you see a situation in a new light? What did you learn from that experience?

Wisdom Questions:

1. Why do you think vulnerability and authenticity are so essential to experiencing true community? What are some of the barriers that can prevent us from opening up to others?

2. Brian talked about the way his focus on his own agenda and desire to prove himself often prevented him from loving his wife well. In what ways can our own selfish ambitions hinder our ability to love and serve others?

3. How can we cultivate a heart that is open to correction and growth in the context of community? What does it look like to invite others to speak the truth into our lives?

Application Questions:

1. Who are the people in your life that you can lean on for support, encouragement, and truth-telling? How can you intentionally cultivate those relationships this week?

2. Is there someone in your life who may be feeling alone or isolated in their journey? How can you reach out to them and extend the love and support of an authentic community?

3. What is one area of your life where you sense God inviting you to growth or healing in the context of community? What practical steps can you take to begin to open up and invite others into that journey with you?

Chapter 8

Embracing the Unfamiliar

Lessons in Telling the Truth

My marriage didn't survive in Guatemala. I know that is a bit of a jump from what I've shared so far, but that's the challenge of sharing my story. It's not just me; it's also about those who've been an important part of my life. So, in this particular area, I'm choosing not to go into the details. I can look back now, and I can see what led to the blowup, and I can start to make sense of things. And I can see my part in that now that I couldn't see at the time. I now understand that there's a benefit to being offended. I don't even belong to myself; I belong to Jesus. But I did not respond well to the struggles of that time. I wish I could say that I leaned into the afflictions of Christ. I wish I could say that I found him in that place of sorrow rather than turning to alcohol. At that moment, I was so mad at God that I couldn't even see him. I didn't think I could trust him anymore, and I don't know what would make me think that it was wise to turn away. But I think it was my anger, and my anger was directed at him.

My deepest prayers now are that trials will turn me more deeply to Jesus and allow him to be my strength and my comfort. I want to be more closely identified with him as a man of sorrow. Sorrows are part of life and what we go through. How we respond to them is what makes a difference in showing who we really are. And I am determined not to walk away again when I face future struggles.

It's much easier to see it from a different angle now that I'm not in the middle of the fire. At the same time, the fire and what I went through taught me that even if we doubt the goodness of God, that doesn't change the fact that he is 100% good. I truly believe he will make all things work for my good in the end. Even when he allows these things to happen to us, it's an opportunity to put to death something that's within us that doesn't belong there anyway. Not that he causes it, but he uses it. And so I have to believe that he's good no matter what and hold on to that. I want to respond more like Jesus, and I need his strength to do it. It's the same as when Jesus said, "Father, forgive them; they know not what they're doing." Or the first martyr, Stephen, said, "They know not what they do." I need to learn forgiveness experientially.

Even when it's going to hurt for a while, I still want to stay and be vulnerable. I want to be honest and let the pain be what it is because the reward is much greater on the other side. I understand that sometimes it takes time to process, and sometimes we've got to be in it, and it takes a little bit for the heart to follow.

I don't know how I would say this well. But basically, if you are married and you want to work through your low points, then you have to determine beforehand what you want to do. You don't leave it up in the air. And if it's something that you want to work through, then go through whatever it takes to get that right, to walk through the woundedness together because love is self-sacrifice. But that is not the path I chose. My path was much more self-destructive.

I had a mentor that I said would tell me like it is. About a year after my divorce, I was in a relationship with a young lady, and he pulled me aside and said, "If you don't quit your crap, you're never going to be useful again. You need to pull your crap together and stop what you're doing immediately." And so he told me the truth where I was at.

Like honestly, the way that I made it through was just a lot of time and more pain. Now, as I look back, God did bring somebody into my life that helped me heal, that saw what I was. This person knew who I truly was before all that happened. And she loved me and put me into the place that I am now. So it's both community that wounds and heals you. It's a paradox.

I'd tell my current wife that I'm a drunk, and she'd say, "You are not a drunk!" She'd never try to control me. But eventually, I could just tell that there's no reason for me to bleed on people that didn't cut you. And so I just stopped bleeding on people.

When I was young and in the world, everybody's always tried to one up everybody else, and I didn't let anybody take advantage of me. So I did whatever it took to not let somebody shame me. My big chip was survival.

When I moved into a different life and came out of that stage and into the Lord, it wasn't about playing the hero role. I learned to just excel at what I do and play the game right. Whatever community I was in, I'd find out what standards I needed to meet, and then I would play according to the rules. Not only that, but I'd leverage my advantages for excellence in ways that nobody else could. My goal was to rise to the second or third from the top. I wanted to be in the inner circle, be one of the guys.

And then, when I was wounded and being picked apart, the chip on my shoulder focused on feeling sorry for myself, doing damage control on my own reputation while acting like I didn't care. In truth, I did care. I wanted people to know that I've suffered and been through a lot.

I ended up back in the middle of Michigan. I was in a small-town Methodist Church, and they had a meal in the basement. I was there with nine or ten 70-year-olds. I started telling them my sad story. I told them about my worries about what had happened to me. All the people there were listening politely and quietly. I thought I had something pretty special to share with them. However, when the next person opened their mouth, I heard 70 years' worth of pain, sorrow, and struggles. By the time the second or third person had laid their narrative on the table, my story was no longer unique, nor did I hold the most pain. That was a way I started hearing the truth, and I saw what others had been through.

I discovered that I wasn't alone and that we all go through some kind of trial.

Now, central to this, to our faith, is Jesus' story. As I said in the introduction, I've been sitting there meditating on the incarnation and the cross and realizing that I've got Christianity wrong.

We grow up in a culture and in a world where everybody's trying to do the best for themselves and looking out for number one even though they call themselves Christians. When I look at the incarnation in the cross, the Kingdom is upside down. The further down you go, the better you see it. The greatest among you is the one who is the servant of all. Unless we come to Jesus as a little child fully dependent, we can't see the Kingdom.

It's not a list of doctrines that we give mental assent to. Jesus is a way of life. The message of the cross is something that we live. It's not just something that we talk about or think about it. He said, "I'm the way the truth and the life." He's a way of life and we enter into his life and he enters into ours.

Kenosis is the emptying of yourself and the process where there's humility before exaltation. But if we're going to follow Jesus, then there needs to be an emptying of ourselves. I'm wrestling with the sovereignty of God and human responsibility. I want to be a servant and actually believe that God will meet all my needs. I'm tempted to make it about doing what I'm supposed to do, meaning I've got to go to work, and I've got to do stuff. But I want to just depend on him, to pray for my daily bread, actually believing that the daily bread comes from him. Because it is God who gives me my health, strength, and ability to perform that job and earn that money, every breath is God's, and everything I do truly depends on him. Without him, I am nothing. And so it comes down to just living that out and realizing and recognizing him as my source 100%. It's so easy to try to take my life back into my own hands.

I want to say a bit more about how it ended in Guatemala. We were in ongoing burnout for two or three years, probably before things fell apart. We were weary, just exhausted from being in another culture, we were not well-grounded with our sending church. Obviously there was a geographical distance, but we were also not fitting in with any local church that was there.

As I look back on my time in Guatemala, I realize that the most important lesson I needed to learn was in the area of truth-telling. Adapting to a new culture, learning a new language, and navigating the complexities of cross-cultural ministry required honesty about my shortcomings. And I wasn't willing to bring that honesty.

I thought it was better and easier to pretend I was the hero. I felt frustrated, overwhelmed, and out of my depth, but I couldn't admit it. Had I been honest about my weakness and inadequacy, I would have encountered the heart of Jesus in a new way. As Philippians 2:5-8 says, "In your relationships with one another, have the same mindset as Christ Jesus: Who, being in very nature God, did not consider equality with God something to be used to his own advantage; rather, he made himself nothing by taking the very nature of a servant, being made in human likeness. And being found in appearance as a man, he humbled himself by becoming obedient to death—even death on a cross!"

Jesus, the King of Kings and Lord of Lords emptied himself and took on the form of a servant. He stepped into our world, our culture, our brokenness, and he loved us with a sacrificial, self-giving love. As I navigated the challenges of cultural adaptation, I failed to see the very heart of the Gospel - not just something to believe, but a way of life to honestly embrace.

Embracing humility would have meant being willing to admit when I was wrong, to ask for help when I needed it, and to lay down my own pride and self-sufficiency. It would have meant learning to serve others not from a place of superiority or pity, but from a place of shared humanity and mutual respect.

So if you find yourself in a place of cultural discomfort or unfamiliarity, if you're wrestling with your own pride and self-sufficiency, I encourage you to embrace the way of Jesus instead of letting it isolate you as it did me. Choose the path of humility and servanthood. Be willing to learn from those around you, to admit when you're wrong, and to lay down your own agenda for the sake of others.

As you do, you'll discover the joy and freedom that comes from walking in the footsteps of our Savior. You'll experience the depth of his love and the power of His transforming grace. And you'll find that even in the most unfamiliar and uncomfortable places, He is with you, guiding you and shaping you into His likeness.

May we be people who embrace the unfamiliar with courage and humility, who serve others with joy and sacrificial love, and who follow Jesus wherever he may lead. For it is in losing our lives that we truly find them, and it is in humbling ourselves that we are lifted up by his grace.

***

Discussion Questions

Coffee Cup Questions:

1. Have you ever experienced culture shock or felt out of place in a new environment? What was that experience like for you, and how did you navigate it?

2. Can you think of a time when someone else's actions or words challenged your cultural assumptions or expectations? What did you learn from that experience?

Wisdom Questions:

1. Why do you think humility is such an essential virtue in cross-cultural ministry (and in the Christian life in general)? What are some of the dangers of pride and self-sufficiency in these contexts?

2. Brian realized that true greatness in God's kingdom is about being loving, sacrificial, and Christ-like. How does this challenge our cul-

tural notions of success and significance?

3. What does it look like to serve others from a place of shared humanity and mutual respect rather than superiority or pity? How can we cultivate this posture in our relationships?

Application Questions:

1. Is there an area of your life where you sense God calling you to greater humility and servanthood? What practical steps can you take this week to embrace that calling?

2. Think about the people in your life who are different from you - whether culturally, socioeconomically, or in some other way. How can you intentionally seek to learn from them and honor their experiences and perspectives?

3. What is one way you can practice sacrificial, Christ-like love and service this week, even if it means setting aside your own comfort or preferences?

Chapter 9

The Rhythm of Rest

Discovering the Power of Sabbath

There was something modeled to me as a staff member at Living Faith. We were asked to do a realignment day once a month, to take 24 hours, and do whatever is life-giving. As an example, it might be to go to the woods, get away from everybody, and just be with God. Look back, look up, and look forward. That was our concept of what Sabbath was. Sometimes, you get a little busy. Even in this season, I do a three-hour Sabbath on a Saturday or Sunday. I look back, I look up, and I look forward. That's the best I've done to this point.

But we didn't take breaks when we were in Guatemala unless we got really tired. There was basically no rhythm to it; it was just go. We knew that it was important to rest, but we didn't make it a priority.

God used to say "rest" to me a lot, and I didn't understand what that meant. Now, in this season, I think I'm starting to grasp it a little bit. When he was telling me to rest, it wasn't necessarily to take a day off. He was telling me to cease striving and stop trying to earn my place. In this culture and in this day, whenever you meet another man, you might say, "Hey, my name is Brian," and they say, "Hey, I'm John." The second question anyone in the world asks is, "What do you do?" Therefore, you're determining one's value or worth by what they do.

So when we start discovering a Sabbath-type thing, it's more grounded in being and who I am before the Lord, letting my doing come out of that and not having to earn anything or add to it. It's just the position of the heart of being at rest in God.

I don't feel like I have anything left to prove; I'm genuinely secure in God and in who I am. I'm fine with what he would have me do or limiting the activities that I am doing. I'm learning to say no in this season. I have said no, and I realize that I'm taking on too much. Recently, I said no and pulled back from one of my involvements. It was a good thing, but it wasn't what I was called to. I hurt somebody's feelings a little bit, but it was good for them, and God will work in and through that. I recognize that I need to be a good husband and a good father first. I need to finish my house before I take care of anything else. I need to enjoy God. Every day is an adventure and an opportunity.

I don't have to create anything special because all of life is ministry. There's not such a thing as sacred and secular. We can dwell in our Garden of Eden right now, walk with him in the garden in the cool of the day, and just enjoy his presence at all times. We don't have to do anything special for God unless he calls us to do a special thing for him. If he does, it's play, not work.

There's a night and day difference from when I was sent out as a missionary to where I am now. The Lord would tell me to "rest," and I even said once to one of my mentors, "God just keeps saying rest. I don't understand." He just kind of looked at me. I don't think he got it either. Maybe he did, but I didn't understand what God was saying then. Now I understand what it is - it's a settledness. It's resting in his bosom, receiving his love, and being deeply satisfied in him.

Just over the weekend, I was enjoying this book called "No Other Foundation" by DeVern Fromke. It was all about the centrality and preeminence of Jesus Christ and ministry unto him versus ministry unto the house or unto others, but letting all your ministry be to him and how life-giving that is. It's the best of his books that I've read.

It reminded me of what prayer is like - being positioned with him from the throne and getting the perspective from where he's at, praying his heart out instead of just being overwhelmed by all the needs of the people. It's about shifting your position, standing with him and having his perspective, saying, "God, do whatever it takes to do it your way," and releasing in prayer to be part of what he decides. Praying in that direction rather than with sympathy which can weigh us down and blind us to the truth sometimes. The book didn't say that specifically, but that's what I got from it.

Intercession, in that sense, is just a different direction of the heart. I think about the story, probably from Wales, where Evan Roberts was crying out "Bend us, bend us!" It's a call to greater breaking, submission - "Move upon my heart and do whatever it is that only you can do."

Rarely do I have a prayer list that I go through when I pray. Ever since going through that season of despair, I listen more than I talk. I just want to be with him. As I'm living my day, it's almost like that Keith Green song, "Make my life a prayer to you."

When I'm going throughout my day, God will put somebody on my heart, and I will reach out to that person. Often, that person will tell me, "I was just going through something," or "Man, I really needed that." Sometimes people have said, "You really hear God. How'd you know?" It happens when I open myself up and then God shows me who needs what.

As I reflect on my journey, I'm struck by how much I've had to learn (and am still learning) about the importance of rest and Sabbath in maintaining a healthy spiritual life. In our fast-paced, achievement-oriented culture, it's so easy to get caught up in the hustle and measure our worth by what we do and how much we accomplish. But God's economy operates on a different value system altogether.

When God first started speaking to me about rest, I didn't fully understand what he meant. I thought it was just about taking a day off here and there, catching my breath when I was tired. But as I've walked with him and experienced the challenges of ministry and life, I've come to realize that rest is so much more than just a break from activity. It's a posture of the heart, a way of being that flows out of our identity in Christ.

In Matthew 11:28-30, Jesus offers this beautiful invitation: "Come to me, all you who are weary and burdened, and I will give you rest. Take my yoke upon you and learn from me, for I am gentle and humble in heart, and you will find rest for your souls. For my yoke is easy, and my burden is light." True rest is found in coming to Jesus, in letting go of our striving and self-effort, and allowing him to carry the weight.

This doesn't mean that we become passive or disengaged from the work God has called us to. Rather, it means that we learn to operate out of a place of abiding in him, letting our doing flow from our being. As Jesus says in John 15:5, "I am the vine; you are the branches. If you remain in me and I in you, you will bear much fruit; apart from me, you can do nothing."

When we learn to rest in God, to find our identity and worth in him alone, it frees us from the tyranny of performance and the pressure to prove ourselves. We can say "no" to things that aren't ours to carry, trusting that God will direct our steps and provide what we need. We can embrace the rhythm of work and rest, knowing that both are gifts from his hand.

This is something I'm still very much learning to live out. It's a daily choice to surrender my agenda and my striving, to trust that God is working even when I'm not. It's a continual invitation to return to that place of abiding, of resting in his love and letting that be the foundation from which I live and serve.

What I'm discovering is that when I do this, when I prioritize rest and Sabbath, not only do I experience greater peace and joy, but I'm actually more fruitful in my work and relationships. I'm able to give out of the overflow of what I'm receiving from God rather than running on empty and striving in my own strength.

So, if you find yourself weary and burdened, or if you're struggling to find rest in the midst of life's demands, can I encourage you to accept Jesus' invitation? Come to him, let him carry the weight, and learn from his gentle and humble heart. Discover the freedom and joy that comes from resting in his love and letting that be the foundation from which you live and serve.

As Psalm 127:2 reminds us, "In vain you rise early and stay up late, toiling for food to eat— for he grants sleep to those he loves." May we be people who know how to rest in the love of God, who understand that our worth is not in what we do but in who we are in Christ. And may we experience the abundant life that comes from abiding in him.

***

Discussion Questions

Coffee Cup Questions:

1. In our busy, achievement-oriented culture, how do you personally struggle with the concept of rest? What makes it challenging for you to slow down and prioritize Sabbath?

2. Can you think of a time when you experienced burnout or exhaustion from overworking or striving? What did you learn from that experience?

Wisdom Questions:

1. Why do you think rest and Sabbath are so countercultural, and why are they so important for our spiritual, emotional, and physical health?

2. How does our understanding of our identity in Christ impact our ability to rest and let go of striving? What does it look like to find our worth in who we are rather than what we do?

3. In what ways can prioritizing rest and Sabbath make us more fruitful and effective in our work and relationships? How have you seen this play out in your own life or in the lives of others?

Application Questions:

1. What is one practical step you can take this week to incorporate more rest and Sabbath into your routine? This could be as simple as setting aside a few hours to unplug and be with God or saying no to an unnecessary commitment.

2. Is there an area of your life where you sense God inviting you to greater rest and abiding in him? What would it look like to surrender your agenda and strife in this area and trust him to carry the weight?

3. How can you cultivate a posture of resting in God's love and letting that be the foundation from which you live and serve? What practices or rhythms can you incorporate into your daily life to help you abide in Christ?

Chapter 10

The Language of the Heart

Cultivating a Life of Prayer

I've been thinking a lot about the Lord's Prayer and how it connects to the present, past, and future. "Give us this day our daily bread" represents the present, focusing on what we need now. It's about looking up to God for our current needs. "Forgive us our debts as we forgive our debtors" is about releasing the past. "Lead us not into temptation and deliver us from the evil one" is a request for the future, aligning our desires with God's and asking for guidance to avoid going down the wrong path.

These three parts are bookended with Kingdom language, "Kingdom come, will be done on Earth as it is in Heaven" and "Yours is the Kingdom, the power and the glory." Then it gives honor to God as the beginning and end. It's a beautiful way to encapsulate the present, past, and future within the prayer.

This insight can change our prayer life. I regularly recite the Lord's Prayer. Sometimes, when I don't know what to pray, I'll pray the Lord's Prayer slowly, really thinking about what I'm saying, really meaning the words that I'm saying to the best of my current understanding. Then I just sit there and think about his humility, the power of God, and how beautiful He is. I realize that if He just said one thing, it would be worth way more than my rambling.

I open myself up to listen, even though doubts creep in, telling me that He won't answer. But he does answer, and the little phrase he says is way more meaningful to me because he asks, "Am I not good?" This question takes me down the memories of every time I've faced my fears in the recent past, and I realize that yes, he is good.

It reminds me of a time when I was in the darkest place, finding comfort in so many other things. I was on the porch, smoking a cigarette, and God asked me, "How do you know that I'm the true God?" I admitted that I didn't know. Then he asked, "How do I feel about you smoking?" I acknowledged that he didn't like it. He pointed out that everything he told me was good for me, right? Life-giving, right? I agreed.

As I sat there and thought about it, I realized that all the things he's ever asked me to do lead to life, peace, goodness, and integrity. There's no gap in that, no unfaithfulness.

I believe that God is way more generous than we know or give him credit for. However, we often don't stop enough to listen or open ourselves up because we don't believe that he's as good as he is. Too many times, we think he's stingy and not generous with his presence and guidance.

What causes us not to hear God's voice? I think it's doubt, pride, and fear. We worry that he might tell us to do something we don't want to do. We don't believe he'll speak, or we don't want him to speak because then we can't be our own god. That's probably the crux of it.

I'm still learning to overcome these obstacles. When I realized that God continually pursued me and that his shoulders were big enough to carry me no matter what I said, did, or where I went, it made a difference. About 40% of the Psalms are laments, and 70% have laments within them, with people complaining about their struggles and then recognizing who God is and walking through that. This helped me believe in his character and love. If he could shoulder all our garbage and still love us, that's when I started sitting more in silence and appreciating him more.

When it comes to portraying something, it's important to be honest and not rush through it. There's a distinction between complaint and lament. Complaint is when we turn our eyes inward, stuck in repetitive victim mode or worry mode. Lament, on the other hand, is when we honestly bring our struggles before God, talking to him about them and letting the truth in our hearts come out. We do this so that he can hold it rather than us holding onto it and going in circles.

Looking back, my life of drinking and drowning in my sorrows was a life of complaint. But when I sat in that Methodist church in Michigan and encountered someone whose story was unlike mine, their faith in the midst of their lament moved me. It started moving me from complaint to lament, sorting it out.

I've learned to be more comfortable with being honest with God. At one point, I was at the furthest, worst, and darkest moment of my life, which wasn't at the time my marriage exploded but a year and a half later. I was ready to end my life. I gave God the most vicious outpouring of my heart, and he loved me at that moment. Even though I didn't realize how pivotal that moment was until years later, I thought to myself, "I can be honest with him."

It changed my world. The greatest barrier to a relationship with God may not be sin in the way we often think of it or immorality; it may be dishonesty. How can you have a relationship with someone when you're keeping something hidden?

Strangely enough, this is what I learned in AA. In the Bible, James talks about confessing your sins to one another so that you may be healed. We evangelicals often focus on the idea that there's only one mediator between God and man, Christ Jesus, and we don't want to do any of that Catholic confession stuff. But there's power in confessing your sin to somebody, seeing their face, and receiving God's forgiveness through another human who says, "I still accept you."

The 4th step in AA is to take a fearless moral inventory, writing down the exact nature of your character defects and the skeletons in your closet. Then, you share it with another human. I found that fear is a toothless tiger when it comes to that. When you release it to another human, even though it's all for God anyway, you don't carry it anymore. It's no longer part of you, and it doesn't haunt you anymore.

I went through some periods where I was on an intellectual journey, exploring a lot of different faiths and perspectives. This was when I was still in prison, trying to find the true faith. I was attempting to make sense of everything and understand where God was in the midst of my struggles.

As I reflect on my journey of learning to cultivate a deeper prayer life and listen to God's voice, a few key principles stand out to me. First and foremost, prayer is about relationship. It's not just about presenting our requests to God or going through a checklist of things we think we should say. It's about engaging in an ongoing, intimate conversation with our Heavenly Father, one that involves both speaking and listening.

One of the most transformative things for me has been learning to approach prayer with honesty and vulnerability. As Hebrews 4:16 encourages us, "Let us then approach God's throne of grace with confidence, so that we may receive mercy and find grace to help us in our time of need." When we come to God with our doubts, our fears, our struggles, and even our anger, we create space for genuine encounter. We invite him into the messy, raw places of our hearts and allow him to meet us there.

This kind of honest prayer requires a deep trust in God's goodness and love. As 1 John 5:14-15 reminds us, "This is the confidence we have in approaching God: that if we ask anything according to his will, he hears us. And if we know that he hears us—whatever we ask—we know that we have what we asked of him." When we truly believe that God is for us and that his heart towards us is good, we can risk being fully known and fully loved.

Another key aspect of deepening our prayer life is learning to listen. So often, we approach prayer as a one-way conversation, but God longs to speak to us as well. As John 10:27 says, "My sheep listen to my voice; I know them, and they follow me." Learning to discern God's voice takes practice and patience. It involves quieting our own thoughts and agendas and creating space for the Holy Spirit to speak.

For me, this often means sitting in silence, meditating on a passage of Scripture, or simply inviting God to speak into my day. It means being attentive to the promptings of the Holy Spirit throughout my daily life, whether that's a sudden thought to reach out to a friend, a sense of conviction about a particular issue, or a word of encouragement that comes to mind. The more we practice listening, the more attuned we become to God's voice.

Finally, developing a deeper prayer life involves consistency and perseverance. Like any relationship, our connection with God grows stronger as we invest time and energy into it. This doesn't mean we have to spend hours on our knees every day (though extended times of prayer can certainly be valuable). It means making prayer a priority weaving it into the fabric of our daily lives.

For me, this looks like starting my day with quiet time with God, inviting him into my work and relationships throughout the day, and ending my day with reflection and thanksgiving. It means being willing to pray even when I don't feel like it, trusting that God is at work.

As we cultivate a lifestyle of prayer, as we learn to engage in honest, vulnerable conversation with God and attune our hearts to his voice, we open ourselves up to a deeper, more transformative relationship with him. We discover, as Jeremiah 33:3 promises, that when we call to him, he will answer us and tell us great and unsearchable things we do not know.

So, if you find yourself longing for a more intimate, authentic prayer life, I encourage you to start where you are. Come to God with your whole heart, holding nothing back. Create space to listen, even if it feels uncomfortable or unfamiliar at first. And commit to the daily, ongoing work of building your relationship with him.

As you do, I believe you'll discover the joy and peace that comes from abiding in his presence. You'll experience the power of prayer to transform not only your own heart but the world around you. And you'll find that no matter what life brings, you have a constant source of strength, wisdom, and love in your Heavenly Father.

***

Discussion Questions

Coffee Cup Questions:

1. What have been some of your biggest struggles or frustrations when it comes to prayer? How have those challenges impacted your prayer life?

2. Can you think of a time when you sensed God speaking to you, whether through a prompting, a scripture, or a word from another person? What was that experience like for you?

Wisdom Questions:

1. Why do you think honesty and vulnerability are so important in our prayer lives? What happens when we try to hide parts of ourselves from God?

2. Brian talks about the difference between complaint and lament. How does understanding this distinction change the way we approach God with our struggles and pain?

3. In what ways can our doubts, fears, and pride hinder us from hearing God's voice? How can we begin to overcome these barriers and cultivate a posture of listening?

Application Questions:

1. What is one practical step you can take to incorporate more listening into your prayer life? This could be setting aside a few minutes of silence, meditating on a passage of scripture, or asking God to highlight someone or something he wants you to pray for.

2. Is there an area of your life where you sense God inviting you to greater honesty and vulnerability in your prayers? What would it look like to bring your whole heart before him in this area?

3. How can you make prayer a more consistent, integrated part of your daily life? Brainstorm some creative ways to remind yourself to pray throughout the day, whether that's setting an alarm, placing a sticky note on your mirror, or finding an accountability partner.

An Important Message

Hey there, I just wanted to take a quick break from my story to say thank you. If you've made it this far, it means you've been walking alongside me through some of the most difficult moments of my life. I am grateful for your willingness to listen and engage with my experiences. In the next few chapters, I'll be going even deeper into the way God restored my life.

If you're finding yourself impacted by what you've read so far, I have a small favor to ask. Would you consider taking a moment to leave an honest review of this book on Amazon? I know it may seem like a small thing, but your words have the power to inspire and encourage countless others who may be on the fence about reading my story.

QR Code for Reviews

By sharing your thoughts, you're not just supporting me and my book, but you're also helping to spread the message of God's unwavering love and intervention. You never know who may come across your review and find the hope and guidance they desperately need.

I understand if you want to wait until you've finished the book, but if you're feeling moved to share now, I would be incredibly grateful. Your review can be a beacon of light for someone else, just as I hope my story has been for you.

Thank you again for being a part of this journey with me. I am truly humbled by your support.

With sincere appreciation,
Brian

Chapter II

The Long Road Home

Encountering Love in Unexpected Places

Well, basically when I came back from Guatemala, I felt that I was abandoned and I was alone. There were a small handful of the church people that were there for me. As is often true during a divorce, there was a lot of pressure to choose to support only one of the parties. My first wife had a much longer history and stronger ties to the church, so that became her place of support. I felt alone.

I went up into the middle of Michigan because I knew my mother and my sister would be there for me. I lived with them for a period, and then I felt like God had me move back to the the Goshen area, to face my fears and to deal with seeing people, places and things I had been avoiding.

I didn't go back to the church that I had been a part of. I wanted my first wife to have that. That was her community and she grew up there since infancy. I was grafted in. If somebody that was close passed away and the funeral was there, I would go to their funeral. It's not that I never went back there, but I never went there to be part of the church again.

In that season, after Guatemala, I couldn't see where God was at.

I thought at one time that those in the Roman Catholic Church weren't saved. I thought that inner healing wasn't good. We just needed to repent and move forward, that type of stuff.

There was a young lady that stayed with us for a while from the US, from Wisconsin, when we were in Guatemala. She was with us for maybe six months or something. She was Roman Catholic, and really loved Jesus. She had a strong relationship with Jesus. Her name was Shannon.

The old habits die hard. She had stayed with us. I tried to be as loving as I could. I was very loving. I cared for Shannon. She was an awesome person, but sometimes I would just get her alone and get the whiteboard out and just have to tell her how she's wrong.

And one day, in the middle of it, the Holy Spirit said, "Is this how she's going to remember you?" And I said, "All right, I'll quit." So I started respecting her faith and her practice and how she grew up. I started walking her to mass every day and we became really good friends.

Even when I came back to visit in Indiana one day, she took a bus from Wisconsin to come to see me and some of my friends. This was after everything had collapsed. I gave her a ride back to the bus stop and told her what had happened.

When I came back from Guatemala, she wrote me a couple of times, like letters, and she would just say things like, "God gives his biggest battles to his strongest soldiers." She was just trying to encourage me. It was really, really nice. She's such a classy, nice person.

On the second letter or third letter, she said, "My parents want to know if you want to go on a retreat." My response was immediate, "Yeah, I'll go on a retreat." So they took me out to some monastery, and it was this big Opus Dei thing. I show up. I don't know anything about Catholicism, except when I was taking her to mass. I learned a little bit then, but not a whole lot.

I show up there, and I'm trying to be kind of veiled. Everybody asked, "So, what parish are you from?" And I'd reply, "Oh, you know, I'm from out in Indiana." They'd ask, "Oh, you know, Father so-and-so?" I'd cautiously reply, "No, not really." I'm just trying to keep my mouth shut because I'm not Catholic, and it's getting really awkward.

For 24 hours, I tried to do the stuff that they were doing, even though I didn't know what they were doing. The morning of the second day, I saw the spiritual director, and I went up to him. I said, "I'm not from a liturgical tradition. I don't really know what's going on." I was like, "Here's what's up. Here's why I'm here." And I just spill my guts to him. At first, he stepped back, and maybe he thought I was an infiltrator or something. But then, after he heard my story, he said, "Well, the last thing that you need is Catholicism. And the last thing that you need is more religion."

He took me to this library, and we walked through it, past all these books. He said, "Oh, there it is," and he pulled the book off the shelf. He said, "This might be a little too radical for some people, but I think it'll be right up your alley." And then he hands me the book by Henri Nouwen called *The Return of the Prodigal*.

He said, "You can go and do the activities with the guys. You can enjoy your time here. You can hang out in your room and read this book. Do whatever you want, whatever you find gives you life. During this time we just want you to know that this place is available to you."

So I took the book and I decided to take him at his word. I went back to my room, and I started reading it. The first page was pure illumination. It was God's presence, speaking to me right where I'm at. I turned the page, and it might just be human writing and didn't connect in the same way. On the next page, God would speak

THE LONG ROAD HOME

to me again. It altered the way that I viewed that story and my understanding of the journey of walking with Christ. That carried me through for a long time. This experience happened in 2017.

It was quite revolutionary, but then, about five years later, it tied in even more strongly. I was married to my second wife, and we are now part of a church called Mission 72. I was pretty new there, and this guy, John Thomas, came to speak at the church. I knew that it was one of the pastor's friends. I wasn't sure what the connection was, but everybody was excited. They said, "Oh, you know, he had spoken here like last year and did this teaching." And so it was a hyped-up moment, but at that point, I was still pretty jaded. My response was, "I don't really care who's speaking or what's going on." At that point, I was just going to church because I felt like I was supposed to do it.

I walk into the church, and as I get through the back doors of the sanctuary I hear the Holy Spirit say, "I've got something for you today." And I thought, "That's nice." So I sat down in the middle near the back.

John Thomas got up and he said, "I've got two messages in my head this morning and I'm not sure which way to go." It almost looks like he spaced out. I mean, that's the only way I know how to describe it. But then it seemed like a light came on. He said, "Oh, there it is."

He started sharing the message about the prodigal son, and it was Nouwen's version. It was the version that I read in the book. I was so overwhelmed in that moment by knowing that there was a man up front preaching the very message that had changed my life in the deepest, darkest place I had been. I was back in the middle of the Catholic monastery where God restored me. Now years later, I was hearing the same message.

When he came to the end, I was so overwhelmed by what had happened. I don't remember everything that was said, but he did say, "If anybody wants..." and then I didn't understand anything else that was being said consciously. All I knew was that whatever he was offering, whatever God was offering, I wanted it. So I stood up. And when I stood up, everything just disappeared.

It was Jesus in front of me. I was just overwhelmed. And then, all of a sudden, I could feel Jesus' love. It's not like talking about his love or saying, "God so loved the world," I fully felt his love! And it was full acceptance. As Jesus was standing up there, it was like these waves, like if you imagine the ocean waves curling, were coming from him. One goes, and then another one hits me, and it's like liquid, warm love. And then the third one came.

By the time the third one hit me, it was like there were these two identities that I was carrying, and they started breaking away, and I could see them in the peripherals being pushed back. It was the young son and the old son, and they were getting broken off. And I was just the beloved. That is what I rest in with everything at this point in life, and that has changed everything I think and know about God: when I was unlovable, he loved me. And that's just it.

As I reflect on my journey of brokenness and redemption, I'm struck by how God met me in the most unexpected places and through the most unlikely people. Growing up in the evangelical tradition, I had a lot of preconceived notions about what it meant to encounter God. I thought it had to happen within the walls of a certain kind of church, through a certain kind of teaching or worship style. But God, in His infinite grace and creativity, had other plans.

When I found myself at that Catholic monastery, broken and desperate for healing, I never imagined that I would find God there. I was an outsider. But in that place of vulnerability and need, God met me through the kindness of a spiritual director who saw past my defenses and pointed me to the heart of the Gospel.

The story of the prodigal son came alive to me in a new way as I read Henri Nouwen's book. I saw myself in both the younger son, who had wandered far from home, and the older son, who had stayed close but harbored bitterness and resentment. And I encountered a Father whose love was big enough to embrace them both, to welcome them home with open arms.

This theme of God's relentless pursuit of love continued to unfold in my life, even as I struggled to find my place in the church. When John Thomas preached that message at Mission 72, it was like God was confirming everything he had been showing me. The words weren't just information; they were an invitation to experience the depth and power of God's love in a tangible way.

As I stood there, feeling wave after wave of God's love washing over me, I realized that this was the love I had been searching for all my life. It wasn't earned or deserved; it was a gift freely given. It had the power to break off the false identities I had been carrying, the labels of "good son" and "bad son," and grounded me in my true identity as a beloved child of God.

This is the heart of the Gospel, the scandalous grace that welcomes sinners home and makes them sons and daughters. As Titus 3:4-5 says, "But when the kindness and love of God our Savior appeared, he saved us, not because of righteous things we had done, but because of his mercy." It's a love that meets us in our worst moments and transforms us from the inside out.

And the beautiful thing is, this love isn't just for me. It's for every person who has ever felt lost, broken, or unworthy. It's for the prodigals and the older brothers, for the insiders and the outsiders. As Romans 5:8 reminds us, "But God demonstrates his own love for us in this: While we were still sinners, Christ died for us."

So, if you find yourself in a place of brokenness or despair, if you feel like you've wandered too far from home to ever be welcomed back, can I just encourage you with this truth? God's love is bigger than your worst moments and your deepest shame. He is always ready to meet you with open arms, to forgive and restore, and to make you new.

And if you've been walking with God for a while but find yourself harboring bitterness or resentment, if you struggle to extend grace to those you deem unworthy, you are also invited to encounter afresh the Father's heart of love. We are all prodigals welcomed home, and we are all recipients of a grace we could never earn.

As we learn to live in light of this love, as we allow it to break off our false identities and ground us in who we truly are in Christ, we become conduits of that love to the world around us. We become people of forgiveness and reconciliation, pointing others to the One who makes all things new.

I hope you encounter the Father's love in fresh ways today, whether in a monastery or a megachurch, through a classic book or a timely sermon. And may you find yourself changed by a love that knows no bounds, a love that leads us home.

***

Discussion Questions

Coffee Cup Questions:

1. Have you ever encountered God in an unexpected place or through an unlikely person? What was that experience like for you?

2. The story of the prodigal son resonates with many people's journeys. Which character in the story do you most identify with, and why?

Wisdom Questions:

1. Why do you think we sometimes limit our understanding of where and how God can meet us? How can we cultivate a posture of openness to His presence in all things?

2. Brian experienced God's love in a tangible, transformative way. How would you describe your own experience of God's love? What has helped you to grasp the depth and breadth of His love for you?

3. Forgiveness and reconciliation are central themes in Brian's story. Why are these things so important in the Christian journey, and what makes them so challenging at times?

Application Questions:

1. Is there an area of your life where you need to experience God's forgiveness and love in a fresh way? Take some time this week to bring that area before Him in prayer, asking Him to meet you there.

2. Is there someone in your life to whom you struggle to extend grace and forgiveness? Ask God to give you His heart for that person and to show you practical ways to demonstrate His love to them.

3. How can you cultivate a greater awareness of God's presence in your daily life, even in the mundane or unexpected moments? Consider starting a practice of "breath prayers" throughout your day, simply whispering a word or phrase of openness and surrender to God.

Chapter 12

The Beauty of Broken Vessels

Finding Healing in Community

I've learned love and acceptance, and what I enjoy about our church is that you can really be yourself. I've seen people get up and say things that might seem shameful, and I've seen people open up and be vulnerable and honest. In response, I've seen people surround them, love them, and pray for them. That's what happened to me. I've seen things as rough as a confession of sin, and then I've seen people gather around them, love them, pray for them, and accept them. Every Sunday, when I come into the building, I don't see a difference in the way that people are treated or looked at because of where they've been or what they've done.

So, I saw something much healthier with more emotional integrity than anything I've ever known. It's kind of like the path is getting better, and as I said, it's almost like the peeling of an onion. My life is like the peeling of an onion because you think that you're good until a layer gets stripped away. But as it's getting closer and closer to the core, you can see the deep roots that have always existed but are unseen because God is making us like him. He's conforming us to the image of Christ, and if we surrender to him, he leaves no stone unturned.

It's all a work of his love, his mercy, and his grace. Even if it looks like failure sometimes, it's falling forward. It's still going forward. A righteous man falls seven times and he gets up. That's the difference between the righteous and the unrighteous - we keep getting back up.

I honestly just put my future hopes in the Lord's hands. Throughout my life, I was taught as a leader to have a vision and all that, but the vision is supposed to come from God. You go up on the mountain like Moses to see the vision, to get an idea of what's going on and how you're going to lead people, but the truth is, I'm not trying to lead anybody.

The one thing that I hope for is what it says in Psalm 27:4: "One thing I ask from the Lord, this only do I seek: that I may dwell in the house of the Lord all the days of my life, to gaze on the beauty of the Lord and to seek him in his temple." That's much better than anything I could possibly do with my life. I don't really have any aspirations, dreams, goals, or hopes other than to see people come to Christ and grow more fully into reflecting him. I want to be more like him, and it's less about what I do and more about who I become.

I just want to be like him, and I want to be honest with him. I want to grow in honesty, both with him and everyone else. I feel like I'm a pretty transparent, vulnerable person, but there's always an element of trying to protect myself. I want to do away with that, but then again, I've got to balance it. Not everybody needs to know all your business, right? There's a difference between transparency and integrity.

There's authority and a role that comes from God, and there's authority and a role that comes from people. I believe that I have a call on my life, but I didn't really want to be in a leadership role at all. I am still trying to pick up the pieces of my life and get myself together. I am still very much broken, but trying to serve people and love people in an everyday capacity, not through any official means.

I recently went through a situation where I saw more clearly that what destroyed my first marriage was something that existed in me as well. I see my first marriage through a whole different lens. God saved me from going through ruin again through strong pastoral care and through the strong hand of my wife. We overcame. My compass was the pastors and brothers that came alongside me. They were both my compass and my shield in so many ways.

My wife Amanda and I help a lot of people. We offer hospitality, and we've loved a lot of people. Through that, we were vulnerable, and I probably wasn't in the healthiest place to be helping somebody. But what I found is through my deepest failures, through my passivity, and through allowing and entertaining things that I shouldn't have, I found pastors who warned me of danger two weeks before it happened. There's no way that they could have known except through prophetic insight from God. I've never been shepherded like that.

And then, with people that were close to me at the church, all the men that I'm friends with, I went and I did my rounds. I told probably half the church, not every detail, but enough that they knew what I felt they needed to know. The information that I gave up front was a little more general, but enough to let everybody know that I sinned and the blame was fully on me.

As I reflect on my experiences at Mission 72 and the profound impact that authentic community has had on my life, I'm reminded of the words of the Apostle Paul in 2 Corinthians 4:7: "But we have this treasure in jars of clay to show that this all-surpassing power is from God and not from us." We are all broken vessels, fragile and flawed, yet chosen by God to carry His presence and love to the world around us.

One of the most beautiful things about being part of a church family is the opportunity to be real, to take off the masks we so often wear, and allow ourselves to be seen and known, even in our brokenness. As James 5:16 instructs us, "Therefore confess your sins to each other and pray for each other so that you may be healed. The prayer of a righteous person is powerful and effective."

I've seen the power of this kind of vulnerability and accountability firsthand. When I found myself in a place of deep brokenness and failure, it was the love and support of my church community that helped me find my way back to wholeness. The pastors and brothers who came alongside me, who spoke truth and grace into my life, were a tangible expression of God's love and care for me.

This isn't to say that vulnerability is easy or comfortable. It requires a level of trust and courage to open up the messy parts of our lives to others. But as Proverbs 28:13 reminds us, "Whoever conceals their sins does not prosper, but the one who confesses and renounces them finds mercy." When we bring our brokenness into the light, when we allow others to see us as we truly are, we create space for God's healing and transformative power to work in us.

As we learn to be vulnerable and authentic with one another, we give others permission to do the same. We create a culture of grace and acceptance, where people feel safe to share their struggles and failures, knowing that they will be met with love and support, not judgment or condemnation.

This is the heart of what it means to be the Church, the Body of Christ. As 1 Corinthians 12:25-26 says, "There should be no division in the body, but that its parts should have equal concern for each other. If one part suffers, every part suffers with it; if one part is honored, every part rejoices with it." We are called to bear one another's burdens, to rejoice with those who rejoice, and mourn with those who mourn.

When we live out this kind of authentic, supportive community, we become a powerful witness to the watching world. We show that the Gospel isn't just about individual salvation but about the transformation of broken lives and the creation of a new family bound together by the love of Christ.

So, if you find yourself in a place of brokenness or struggle, I encourage you to lean into the power of community. Seek out trusted brothers and sisters in Christ who can walk alongside you, pray for you, and speak truth into your life. Don't let shame or fear keep you isolated and alone. You were made for relationships, and it's in the context of authentic community that we find healing and wholeness.

And if you're on the other side, if you find yourself in a place of strength and stability, I challenge you to be a safe place for others. Look for opportunities to extend grace, to offer a listening ear and a supportive presence. Be quick to forgive, slow to judge, and always ready to point others to the hope and healing found in Christ.

As we learn to live out this vision of an authentic, vulnerable community, as we allow ourselves to be broken vessels filled with the treasure of God's love, I believe we'll see lives transformed and the world impacted in powerful ways. May we be a church that celebrates the beauty of broken vessels, that creates space for healing and growth, and that shines the light of Christ in a world desperate for hope.

***

Discussion Questions

Coffee Cup Questions:

1. Can you think of a time when you experienced an authentic, supportive community in a church or small group setting? What made that experience meaningful to you?

2. Vulnerability and accountability can be challenging for many of us. What are some of the barriers that keep you from opening up and sharing your struggles with others?

Wisdom Questions:

1. Why do you think vulnerability and authenticity are so essential to experiencing true healing and growth in our spiritual lives? What happens when we try to hide or protect ourselves?

2. Brian talks about the importance of having people in our lives who can speak truth and grace to us, even when it's uncomfortable. Who are those people for you, and how have they impacted your journey?

3. The Bible talks about the Church as a body, where every part has a role to play and a responsibility to care for others. What do you think this looks like in practice? How can we cultivate a culture of mutual support and care in our church communities?

Application Questions:

1. Is there an area of brokenness or struggle in your life that you've been hesitant to share with others? What would it look like to take a step towards vulnerability this week, whether that's with a trusted friend, a small group, or a pastor?

2. Think about the people in your church community. Is there someone who you sense may be going through a difficult time and could use some extra support? Reach out to them this

week, whether it's with a text, a phone call, or an invitation to coffee.

3. How can you use your own experiences of brokenness and healing to encourage and support others who may be struggling? Look for opportunities to share your story and point others to the hope and healing found in Christ.

Chapter 13

The Unfinished Story

Lessons in Redemption and Grace

When I was sixteen or seventeen, I was living at my dad's house up in Union, Michigan. All I would do is get drunk, smoke weed, and do drugs all the time. I thought I was a pretty worthless individual. During that time, I was sleeping one night, and in my dream, a man came to me. He had a bright face, and he said, "Get up. I have something for you to do today. Get your brother and sister ready for school. You're going to go to work with your dad."

I woke up, and it wasn't like waking up. I just opened my eyes because it was so real. I got up and started picking up the house, and I got my brother and sister off to school. I sat on the couch and waited for my dad to get up. Whenever he woke up, he looked at me like, "What are you doing up?" I said, "I'm going to go to work with you today." He said, "Alright." So I jumped in the truck with him.

We drove from Union, Michigan down to a gas station in Goshen, Indiana. As I sat in the truck, I thought, "What am I doing here?" Then I heard the voice say, "Inside." So I got out of the truck and went into the gas station. As I stood there, I looked around trying to figure out why I was in there. There were three or four people and my eyes locked with a young man about my age.

I approached this young man, having no idea what I'm going to say. As I get close, out of my mouth come the words, "Are you hungry?" He looked at me afraid, and shook his head yes. Then the words come out of my mouth, "Come with me."

He came out and got into the truck with us. My dad looked back in the rearview mirror, and I told him, "I think we have to go home, Dad." He drove us forty minutes out of the way back up to Michigan. I don't know if he thought I was up to some shenanigans or what, but he drove us up there.

I started making some breakfast, some eggs for the young man. We were living in an open concept modular house where you could see the living room from the kitchen. As I made his omelet, I heard violent sobbing in the living room. I finished making his food and brought it out to him. He starts crying out, "You don't understand. You don't understand."

I was trying to comfort him and hand him food. He said that at 3:30 in the morning, he had broken into an abandoned house because he thought he was going to freeze. He said, "I told God if he gave me a warm place to go and something to eat, that I'd give him my life forever. You're an angel. You're an angel." I told him I wasn't an angel.

Then I went and proceeded to do my daily activities of getting some money together so I could get some beer and get drunk. Later on, my dad came home and took him somewhere. So God intervened in my life, visited me in a dream, and used me to help someone else before I really admitted to knowing him.

The second time was when I was running from the police for nine months or maybe a year. I was sitting on the porch, living with my friend, and I started drinking like I did every day. As I was sitting on the porch, drinking, a cop looked like he was going to drive by. Suddenly, he whipped the car around and skidded to a stop in the yard. He came up to me and said, "What's your name?" I made up a name, but he knew who I was. He arrested me.

The night before, I had a dream where the Lord came to me and said, "If you don't quit, you're going to die." I woke up and sat on the end of my bed and said, "Well, make me quit." The cops arrested me the next morning. He made me quit. I told him, "Make me quit." I wanted to, but I couldn't quit on my own. He made me quit.

What do I hope people take away from my story? God sees you, and he hears you, no matter where you're at. You're not far away from him. There's no place that you could flee from his presence. He is way more for you than you could ever imagine. If you could just trust in that, you'll fare well.

These two dreams I experienced at different points in my life highlight an important truth: God is always at work, even before we recognize it. He's constantly inviting us into his Kingdom work and warning us when we need to change course. Our brokenness, our failures, and our struggles do not prevent us from having a relationship with him. In fact, it's often in those very places of weakness and desperation that we encounter his grace most powerfully.

In the first dream, God used me to minister to a young man in need, even though I was far from living a life that honored him. He saw beyond my sin and brokenness and chose to involve me in his plan to show love and compassion to a stranger. This reminds me of the truth that God doesn't call the qualified; he qualifies the called. Our worth and usefulness to God aren't based on our perfection but on his grace and the transforming power of his Spirit within us.

The second dream served as a warning, a wake-up call to the destructive path I was on. God, in his mercy, was reaching out to me, urging me to turn from my self-destructive ways and turn to him. Even in my rebellion and disobedience, he was pursuing me, not willing to let me go without a fight. This is the relentless love of our Heavenly Father, who leaves the ninety-nine to go after the one lost sheep.

As I reflect on my journey and the lessons I've learned along the way, I'm struck by the incredible patience and faithfulness of God. No matter how far I strayed or how many times I stumbled, he never gave up on me. His love remained constant, his grace sufficient for each new day.

One of the most important things I've come to understand is that following Jesus isn't about perfection or performance; it's about surrender and obedience. It's about daily taking up our cross, dying to our own desires and agendas, and allowing Christ to live his life through us. This isn't a one-time event but a lifelong process of growth and transformation.

I've also learned the value of community and accountability. We were never meant to walk this path alone. We need brothers and sisters who will encourage us, challenge us, and speak truth into our lives. We need to be willing to be vulnerable and honest about our struggles, knowing that there is healing and freedom in bringing our brokenness into the light.

Another key lesson has been the importance of humility. The more I've grown in my faith, the more I've realized how much I don't know and how desperately I need God's wisdom and guidance. Pride is a subtle but deadly poison that can creep in and destroy our relationship with God and others. But when we embrace humility, when we recognize our own limitations and depend wholly on God, we open ourselves up to receive His grace and power in new and profound ways.

Finally, I've discovered that the Christian life is not about striving for some unattainable standard of holiness but about resting in the finished work of Christ. It's about learning to abide in him, to draw our strength and life from His presence within us. As we do this, we find that his grace truly is sufficient and that his power is made perfect in our weakness.

I want to say this as clearly as I can: no matter where you find yourself on your journey, no matter how broken or lost you may feel, know that God sees you, he hears you, and he is for you. He is always at work, always inviting you into a deeper relationship with him. Your brokenness does not disqualify you from his love; in fact, it's the very thing that can lead you to the foot of the cross, where true healing and transformation begin.

Don't be afraid to take up your cross daily and follow him. The path may be narrow and difficult at times, but it leads to life - abundant, eternal, and overflowing with the goodness and grace of God. Trust in his faithfulness, lean into his love, and let him write his story of redemption in and through your life.

My prayer is that as you reflect on the lessons and truths shared in these pages, you will be encouraged and inspired to press on in your own journey of faith. May you discover, as I have, that in the midst of our brokenness and pain, God is always at work, always redeeming, always transforming us into the image of his Son. May you find, in the depths of your heart, the courage and strength to say "yes" to his invitation each and every day.

***

Discussion Questions

Coffee Cup Questions:

1. Brian's story is one of redemption and grace, with God meeting him in his darkest moments. Can you recall a time in your own life when you experienced God's presence or intervention in a profound way?

2. In this chapter, Brian shares two powerful dreams that highlight God's active role in his life. Have you ever had a dream or experience

that you felt was a message or guidance from God? How did it impact you?

Wisdom Questions:

1. Throughout his journey, Brian learned that God was always present, even in the midst of his brokenness and struggles. How can we cultivate a greater awareness of God's presence in our daily lives, especially during challenging times?

2. Brian's story illustrates the truth that our past does not define our future and that God's redemptive power can transform even the most broken situations. How can we hold onto hope and trust in God's redemptive plan when we face difficult circumstances or feel weighed down by our past?

3. The chapter concludes with Brian's realization that God is always for us and that trusting in His goodness is the key to navigating life's ups and downs. In what areas of your life do you find it challenging to trust in God's goodness, and how can you grow in this area?

Application Questions:

1. Brian's experiences with God often involved surrender and obedience, even when it was difficult or didn't make sense. Is there an area of

your life where you sense God calling you to surrender or obedience? What practical steps can you take to respond to that call?

2. The chapter encourages us to remember that God is always with us and hears our prayers, no matter where we find ourselves. How can you make prayer a more consistent and integral part of your daily life, and what reminders or practices can help you stay connected to God's presence?

3. Brian's story is a powerful testimony of God's transformative love and grace. How can you share your own story of God's work in your life with others, and who might benefit from hearing about the hope and redemption you've experienced?

***

My Gratitude for You

I hope that you've been blessed by my story and the way God has worked in my life. If my experiences have touched you in some way, I would be truly grateful if you could share your thoughts in an Amazon review. Your honest reflections could be the encouragement someone else needs to read my story and find hope in their own struggles.

By leaving a review, you have the power to inspire others who are eager to grow and be transformed. Your words can be the catalyst that helps them take the next step in their journey with God. You never know the impact your perspective can have on countless lives.

QR Code for Reviews

Thank you for being a part of sharing my story. Your support helps extend the reach of how God can change every human heart and life, no matter how lost or broken we may feel. If you would, please take a moment right now to go to Amazon, find my book, and leave your review.

I am truly grateful for your willingness to contribute in this way. Thank you for joining me in this mission to spread the message of God's love and intervention.

With heartfelt appreciation,
Brian

Made in the USA
Monee, IL
01 July 2024